175

# Mind Puzzlers

### George J. Summers

 Sterling Publishing Co., Inc. New York

**Library of Congress Cataloging in Publication Data**

Summers, George J.
  Mind puzzlers.

  Includes index.
    1. Puzzles.   2. Detective and mystery stories.
  I. Hoffman, Sanford.   II. Title.
  GV1507.D4S86   1984      793.7'3      83-24291
  ISBN 0-8069-4684-9
  ISBN 0-8069-7842-2 (pbk.)
Second Printing, 1985
Copyright © 1984 by George J. Summers
Published by Sterling Publishing Co., Inc.
Two Park Avenue, New York, N.Y. 10016
Distributed in Australia by Oak Tree Press Co., Ltd.
P.O. Box K514 Haymarket, Sydney 2000, N.S.W.
Distributed in the United Kingdom by Blandford Press
Link House, West Street, Poole, Dorset BH15 1LL, England
Distributed in Canada by Oak Tree Press Ltd.
% Canadian Manda Group, P.O. Box 920, Station U
Toronto, Ontario, Canada M8Z 5P9
*Manufactured in the United States of America*

# Table of Contents

# Introduction

The puzzles in this book have been composed to resemble short whodunits. Each puzzle contains some "clues" and it is up to the reader, as "detective," to determine from these "clues" which of the various "suspects" is the "culprit."

The general method for solving these puzzles is as follows:

The question presented at the end of each puzzle contains a condition that must be satisfied by the solution. For example, "Who spoke?" contains the condition "spoke."

The "clues" numbered when there are more than one, also contain conditions; these conditions concern the various "suspects." The "detective" must use all of the conditions to determine the unique "culprit" that satisfies the condition contained in the question. In general, a solution is reached by reasoning which eliminates the impossible situations until only the correct situation remains.

A Solution Scheme is provided for each of 34 puzzles to help the reader relate the puzzle to its solution. Two of the puzzles have no Solution Scheme because of their unusual nature (see Preface); a Hint is offered instead. In addition, each puzzle after the first is given a Classification that tells the reader which of five concepts are involved in the puzzle (see Preface).

# Preface

If you've ever seen a puzzle labeled "logic problem," it was probably like this one:

Pam, Ray, Sue, and Tom are an archeologist, a botanist, a chiropractor, and a dentist—though not necessarily in that order. At a party Tom said to the botanist that Sue would be along in a minute, the chiropractor congratulated the dentist on his engagement to Sue, and Pam took a picture of the chiropractor standing next to Ray. What is the occupation of each person?

With the exception of the first puzzle in this book, which is a variation on the matching exercise above, none of the puzzles in this book is like that one.

After the first puzzle, each Mind Puzzler in this book involves one or more of the following:

### STATEMENTS THAT MAY BE FALSE

Statements may be false because the people who make them always lie, sometimes lie, lie only at certain times, or alternately tell the truth and lie; they may be false because the people who make them are simply incorrect in what they believe to be true or in what they predict to be true; or they may be false because one of a given number of statements is said to be false, or all but one of a given number of statements are said to be false.

### STATEMENTS BEGINNING WITH "IF"

A statement that contains *if* has a hypothesis and a conclusion, as in:

If I stay home tonight, then I will watch TV.

The hypothesis is: "If I stay home tonight"
The conclusion is: "then I will watch TV."
What is meant by saying this statement is true?
To answer this question: Suppose I don't stay home tonight. Then I am free to do whatever I want, including watching TV or not watching TV. So a false hypothesis does not make the statement false; that is, the statement is still true. So

the statement is true when the hypothesis is false
and the conclusion is true

the statement is true when the hypothesis is false
and the conclusion is false

Suppose I do stay home tonight. Then, in order for the statement to be true, I must watch TV. Otherwise, the statement is false. So

the statement is true when the hypothesis is true
and the conclusion is true

the statement is false when the hypothesis is true
and the conclusion is false

A statement that contains a hypothesis and a conclusion can be called a hypothetical statement. When a hypothetical statement is true, you cannot tell whether the hypothesis is true or whether the conclusion is true. However, when a hypothetical statement is false, you know immediately that the hypothesis is true and the conclusion is false. Here is an example of a puzzle containing statements that begin with "if."

[1] If Natalie is married, then Marlene is not married.

[2] If Natalie is not married, then Loretta is married.

[3] If Marlene is married, then Loretta is not married.

Whose marital status do you know?

*SOLUTION:* Suppose Marlene is married. Then, from [1], Natalie is not married (otherwise, Marlene is not married) and, from [3], Loretta is not married. Then from [2], Natalie is married (otherwise, Loretta is married). Then Natalie is both married and not married. This situation is impossible. So *you know Marlene's marital status*: Marlene is not married. Then: if Natalie is not married, then Loretta is married; if Natalie is married, then you don't know whether Loretta is or not. So *you know only Marlene's marital status.*

## "SUSPECTS" ASSOCIATED WITH A STRAIGHT OR A CYCLIC ORDER— A ONE-DIMENSIONAL ASSOCIATION

Straight orders include: arrival times of people at a mansion, a sequence of eliminated words paralleling a sequence of given information, ages of people, players' turns in a game, tennis-playing abilities of people, west-to-east locations of peoples' apartments, and the order in which entrants finish a race.

Cyclic orders include: a playing arrangement of people around a tennis court, a seating arrangement of people around a table, and days of the week.

A special use of ordering involves someone knowing something from the fact that someone else knows or doesn't know something. Here is an example:

[1] After being blindfolded and hatted, two men—Xavier and Yoeman—are truthfully told that either they each wear black hats or one wears a black hat and the other wears a red hat.

[2] After the blindfolds are removed, first Xavier and then Yoeman is asked to name the color of the hat on his head.

[3] The question is repeated until one man says truthfully that he does not have enough information to know the color of his hat.

Who never knows the color of his hat?

SOLUTION: Suppose Yoeman has a red hat. Then, from [1] and [2], Xavier declares he has a black hat. Then, from [1] and [2], Yoeman declares he has a red hat (because Xavier knew his color). From [3], this situation is impossible. So, from [1], Yoeman has a black hat. Then from [1] and [2], Xavier declares he doesn't know. Then, from [1] and [2], Yoeman declares he has a black hat for one of two reasons: (1) Yoeman sees a red hat on Xavier; (2) Yoeman sees a black hat on Xavier and knows that Xavier would have known the color of his hat if he had seen a red hat on Yoeman; because Xavier didn't know, Yoeman knows he has a black hat. So, because Xavier doesn't know which of the reasons Yoeman had for knowing the color of his (Yoeman's) hat, *Xavier never knows the color of his (Xavier's) hat.*

Two puzzles in this book are of this "unusual nature," as mentioned in the Introduction.

## "SUSPECTS" ASSOCIATED BY BLOOD TIES OR WITH VARIOUS PARTS OF A REGION— A TWO-DIMENSIONAL ASSOCIATION

Blood ties include:

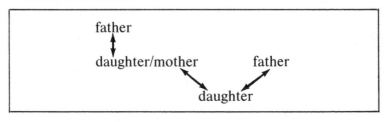

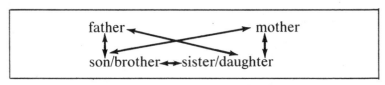

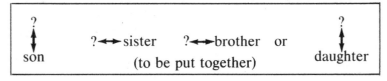

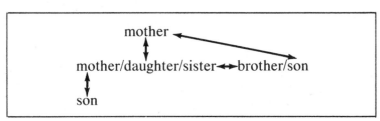

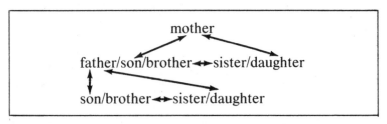

Note that each line in a chart above represents a generation, and that each person is related to the others in a chart in various ways (though relationships such as son-in-law or aunt are not shown); thus, a two-dimensional picture emerges.

Regional relationships include faces of a cube, a layout of rooms, a game board, a cross-number diagram, and a layout of cards.

## A SOLUTION THAT USES COMPUTATION WITH GIVEN QUANTITIES—A MATHEMATICAL SOLUTION

Quantities include: multiples of numbers, numbers of people, digits in arithmetic, numbers in a cross-number diagram, numbers of physical traits, points scored in a game, numbers on discs, and numbers of correct predictions.

In summary, in a puzzle

(1) statements
may be
(a) false
(b) hypothetical

(2) suspects may be
involved in an
association that is
(a) one-dimensional
(b) two-dimensional

(3) the solution
may use
mathematics

Each puzzle after the first is given a Classification by abbreviating the five ideas discussed above, placing the abbreviations in a chart, and inserting check marks in the appropriate columns. For example,

| Statements | | Association | | |
|------|------|--------|--------|------|
| false | hyp. | 1-dim. | 2-dim. | Math. |
| | ✔ | | ✔ | |

# Vera's Preference

Vera prefers her dates to be tall, dark, and handsome.

[1] Of the preferred traits—tall, dark, and handsome—no two of Adam, Boyd, Cary, and Dirk have the same number.

[2] Only Adam or Dirk is tall and fair.

[3] Only Boyd or Cary is short and handsome.

[4] Adam and Cary are either both tall or both short.

[5] Boyd and Dirk are either both dark or both fair.

Who is tall, dark, and handsome?

*Solution Scheme, page 14;*
*Solution, page 86.*

# Speaking of Tennis

Four people played a tennis game.

[1] The four people were Winifred, her father, her husband, and their daughter.

After the game, one of them spoke truthfully about one time during the game:

[2] "I was directly across the net from the server's daughter.

[3] My partner (on the same side of the net as I) was directly across the net from the receiver's father.

[4] The server was diagonally across the net from the receiver (of course)."

Who spoke?

*Classification and Solution Scheme, page 15; Solution, page 86.*

# Vera's Preference

*SOLUTION SCHEME*

Make a chart for yourself as follows:

|            | Is Adam | Is Boyd | Is Cary | Is Dirk |
|-----------:|---------|---------|---------|---------|
| tall?      |         |         |         |         |
| dark?      |         |         |         |         |
| handsome?  |         |         |         |         |

Write "yes" or "no" in each box so that no condition is contradicted.

# Speaking of Tennis

*CLASSIFICATION*

| Statements | | Association | | |
|---|---|---|---|---|
| false | hyp. | 1-dim. | 2-dim | Math. |
| | | ✔ | ✔ | |

*SOLUTION SCHEME*

Make a diagram for yourself as follows:

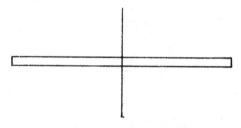

Write "Winifred," "her father," "her husband," or "their daughter" in each of the four parts of the tennis court diagram and write "server" or "receiver" in each of two parts so that no condition is contradicted.

# Getting Married

Four men—Aaron, Barry, Colin, and David—and four women—Marie, Norma, Olive, and Pearl—attended a wedding.

[1] One of the four men married one of the four women.

[2] If Aaron did not get married and if Marie did not get married, then Olive got married.

[3] If Aaron did not get married and if Norma did not get married, then Barry got married.

[4] If Barry did not get married and if Olive did not get married, then Colin got married.

[5] If Colin did not get married and if Norma did not get married, then Marie got married.

Who got married?

*Classification and Solution Scheme, page 18; Solution, page 87.*

# My House Number

My house has a number.

[1] If my house number is a multiple of 3 ($0 \times 3$, $1 \times 3$, $2 \times 3$, etc.), then it is a number from 50 through 59.

[2] If my house number is not a multiple of 4, then it is a number from 60 through 69.

[3] If my house number is not a multiple of 6, then it is a number from 70 through 79.

What is my house number?

*Classification and Solution Scheme, page 19. Solution, page 88.*

# Getting Married

| Statements | | Association | | |
|---|---|---|---|---|
| false | hyp. | 1-dim. | 2-dim. | Math. |
| | ✔ | | | |

## SOLUTION SCHEME

Make a chart for yourself as follows:

| | married Marie | married Norma | married Olive | married Pearl |
|---|---|---|---|---|
| Aaron | | | | |
| Barry | | | | |
| Colin | | | | |
| David | | | | |

Place an "X" in one box so that no condition is contradicted.

# My House Number

| Statements | | Association | | |
|---|---|---|---|---|
| false | hyp. | 1-dim. | 2-dim. | Math. |
| | ✔ | | | ✔ |

SOLUTION SCHEME

Make a chart for yourself as follows:

My house number is

| 50 | 51 | 52 | 53 | 54 | 55 | 56 | 57 | 58 | 59 |
|---|---|---|---|---|---|---|---|---|---|
| 60 | 61 | 62 | 63 | 64 | 65 | 66 | 67 | 68 | 69 |
| 70 | 71 | 72 | 73 | 74 | 75 | 76 | 77 | 78 | 79 |

Cross off every number that contradicts any condition.

# The Murderer in the Mansion

The owner of the mansion has been murdered! The visitors to the mansion were Allen, Bixby, and Crain.

[1] The murderer, who was one of the three visitors, arrived at the mansion later than at least one of the other two visitors.

[2] A detective, who was one of the three visitors, arrived at the mansion earlier than at least one of the other two visitors.

[3] The detective arrived at the mansion at midnight.

[4] Neither Allen nor Bixby arrived at the mansion after midnight.

[5] The earlier arriver of Bixby and Crain was not the detective.

[6] The later arriver of Allen and Crain was not the murderer.

Who was the murderer?

*Classification and Solution Scheme, page 22.*
*Solution, page 88.*

# The Cube

     [1]           [2]           [3]

Three views of the same cube are shown above.

Which of the five letters—E, H, I, N, or S—occurs twice on the cube?

*Classification and Solution Scheme, page 23.*
*Solution, page 89.*

# The Murderer in the Mansion

CLASSIFICATION

| Statements | | Association | | |
|---|---|---|---|---|
| false | hyp. | 1-dim. | 2-dim. | Math. |
| | | ✔ | | |

*SOLUTION SCHEME*

Make a chart for yourself as follows:

| | arrived before midnight | arrived at midnight | arrived after midnight |
|---|---|---|---|
| Allen | | | |
| Bixby | | | |
| Crain | | | |
| The murderer | | | |
| The detective | | | |

Place an "X" in each of five boxes so that no condition is contradicted.

# The Cube

*CLASSIFICATION*

| Statements | | Association | | |
| --- | --- | --- | --- | --- |
| false | hyp. | 1-dim. | 2-dim. | Math. |
| | | | ✔ | |

*SOLUTION SCHEME*

Draw a multiview cube as shown below:

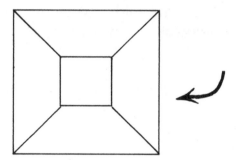

Place "E," "H," "I," "N," or "S" on each face of this multiview cube and at the arrow (to indicate the only face not seen) so that no condition is contradicted.

# Three-Letter Word

Here is a list of words:

INN    PEN    PET    PIE    TEE    TIE

[1] Three logicians are told, "I have told each of you one of the three letters in a word listed before you so that the three known letters together spell the word."

[2] Then they are told, "None of you can tell how many vowels the word has."

[3] Then they are told, "At this point still none of you can tell how many vowels the word has."

[4] Then one of the three logicians says he knows what the word is.

What is the word?

*Classification and Solution
Scheme, page 26;
Solution, page 90.*

# Esther's Fiancé

Esther is engaged.

[1] Her fiancé is either Arthur, Barton, Claude, or Dexter.

[2] Each of the four men and Esther either always tells the truth or always lies.

[3] Arthur says: "Exactly one of us four men always tells the truth."

[4] Barton says: "Exactly one of us four men always lies."

[5] Claude says: "Arthur or Barton is Esther's fiancé."

[6] Esther says: "My fiancé and I either both always tell the truth or both always lie."

Who is Esther's fiancé?

*Classification and Solution*
*Scheme, page 27;*
*Solution, page 90.*

# Three-Letter Word

| Statements | | Association | | |
| --- | --- | --- | --- | --- |
| false | hyp. | 1-dim. | 2-dim. | Math. |
| | | ✔ | | |

*SOLUTION SCHEME*

Make a chart for yourself as follows:

| After the declaration was made in | none of the three logicians could have been told the word had a(n) | | | | |
| --- | --- | --- | --- | --- | --- |
| | E | I | N | P | T |
| [2] | | | | | |
| [3] | | | | | |

Place an "X" in one box of each row so that no condition is contradicted.

# Esther's Fiancé

*CLASSIFICATION*

| Statements | | Association | | |
|---|---|---|---|---|
| false | hyp. | 1-dim. | 2-dim. | Math. |
| ✔ | | | | |

*SOLUTION SCHEME*

Make a chart for yourself as follows:

| | always tells the truth | always lies |
|---|---|---|
| Arthur | | |
| Barton | | |
| Claude | | |
| Dexter | | |
| Esther's fiancé | | |

Place an "X" in one box in each row so that no condition is contradicted.

# Family Occupations

One of four people is a singer and another is a dancer.

[1] The four people are Mr. Brown, his wife, their son, and their daughter.

[2] If the singer and the dancer are the same sex, then the dancer is older than the singer.

[3] If neither the singer nor the dancer is the parent of the other, then the singer is older than the dancer.

[4] If the singer is a man, then the singer and the dancer are the same age.

[5] If the singer and the dancer are of opposite sex, then the man is older than the woman.

Whose occupation do you know?

*Classification and Solution Scheme, page 30; Solution, page 91.*

# A Small Party

"At the party:

[1] There were 9 men and children.

[2] There were 2 more women than children.

[3] The number of different man-woman couples possible was 24. (If there were 10 men and 5 women at the party, then there would have been 10 × 5 or 50 man-woman couples possible.)

Of the three groups—men, women, and children—at the party:

[4] There were 4 of one group.

[5] There were 6 of one group.

[6] There were 8 of one group."

[7] Exactly one of the speaker's statements is false.

Which of [1] through [6] is false?

*Classification and Solution*
*Scheme, page 31;*
*Solution, page 91.*

# Family Occupations

| Statements | | Association | | |
|---|---|---|---|---|
| false | hyp. | 1-dim. | 2-dim. | Math. |
| | ✔ | ✔ | ✔ | |

*SOLUTION SCHEME*

Make a chart for yourself as follows:

| Singer | Dancer |
|---|---|
| | |
| | |
| | |

Write "Mr. Brown," "his wife," "their son," or "their daughter" in each box in as many ways as possible—crossing off any unused boxes—so that no condition is contradicted.

# A Small Party

CLASSIFICATION

| Statements | | Association | | |
|---|---|---|---|---|
| false | hyp. | 1-dim. | 2-dim. | Math. |
| ✔ | | | | ✔ |

*SOLUTION SCHEME*

Make a chart for yourself as follows:

| | men | women | children |
|---|---|---|---|
| Number of | | | |

Write a number in each box so that no condition is contradicted.

# The Separated Couple

Mr. and Mrs. Alden, Mr. and Mrs. Brent, Mr. and Mrs. Crown, and Mr. and Mrs. Drake were seated around a table.

[1] Their chairs were arranged around the square table like this:

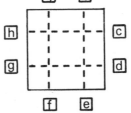

[2] The person sitting across from Mrs. Alden was a man who sat on Mr. Brent's immediate left.

[3] The person sitting on Mrs. Crown's immediate left was a man who sat across from Mr. Drake.

[4] Only one couple did not sit next to each other and this couple did not sit across from each other.

Which couple did not sit next to each other?

*Classification and Solution Scheme, page 34; Solution, page 92.*

# The Opposite Sex

Carmen, Evelyn, Leslie, and Marion are related.

[1] Carmen or Evelyn is Leslie's only son.

[2] Evelyn or Leslie is Marion's sister.

[3] Marion is Carmen's brother or only daughter.

[4] One of the four is the opposite sex from each of the other three.

Who is the opposite sex from each of the others?

*Classification and Solution Scheme, page 35; Solution, page 93.*

# The Separated Couple

*CLASSIFICATION*

| Statements | | Association | | |
|---|---|---|---|---|
| false | hyp. | 1-dim. | 2-dim. | Math. |
| | | ✔ | | |

*SOLUTION SCHEME*

Make a diagram for yourself as follows:

Using the symbols $M_A$ for Alden man, $W_A$ for Alden woman, etc., place the Aldens, Brents, Crowns, and Drakes around the table so that no condition is contradicted.

# The Opposite Sex

*CLASSIFICATION*

| Statements | | Association | | |
|---|---|---|---|---|
| false | hyp. | 1-dim. | 2-dim. | Math. |
| | | | ✔ | |

*SOLUTION SCHEME*

Make a chart for yourself as follows:

| | Leslie's only son | Marion's sister | Carmen's brother | Carmen's only daughter |
|---|---|---|---|---|
| Carmen is | | | ///// | ///// |
| Evelyn is | | | | |
| Leslie is | ///// | | | |
| Marion is | | ///// | | |

Place an "X" in each of three boxes so that no condition is contradicted.

# Truth Day

Philip lies a lot.

[1] He tells the truth only on one of the days of the week.

[2] The days of the week in order are: Sunday, Monday, Tuesday, Wednesday, Thursday, Friday, Saturday, Sunday, Monday, etc.

[3] One day he said: "I lie on Mondays and Tuesdays."

[4] The next day he said: "Today is either Thursday, Saturday, or Sunday."

[5] The next day he said: "I lie on Wednesdays and Fridays."

On which day of the week does Philip tell the truth?

*Classification and Solution Scheme, page 38; Solution, page 93.*

# The Murderer in the Hotel

Arlene, Brenda, Cheryl, Daniel, Emmett, and Farley stayed in a hotel.

[1] Each stayed in a different one of six rooms as shown here:

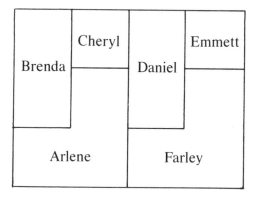

[2] One of the six murdered one of the other five.

[3] If the murderer and the victim stayed in rooms that did not border on each other, then Arlene or Farley was the victim.

[4] If the murderer and the victim stayed in rooms that bordered on different numbers of rooms, then Brenda or Cheryl was the murderer.

[5] If the murderer and the victim stayed in rooms that were different in size, then Daniel or Emmett was the murderer.

Who was the murderer?

*Classification and Solution Scheme, page 39;*
*Solution, page 94.*

# Truth Day

*CLASSIFICATION*

| Statements | | Association | | |
| --- | --- | --- | --- | --- |
| false | hyp. | 1-dim. | 2-dim. | Math. |
| ✔ | | ✔ | | |

*SOLUTION SCHEME*

Make a chart for yourself as follows:

| | Sun | Mon | Tues | Wed | Thurs | Fri | Sat |
| --- | --- | --- | --- | --- | --- | --- | --- |
| Declaration in [3] was made on a: | | | | | | | |
| Declaration in [4] was made on a: | | | | | | | |
| Declaration in [5] was made on a: | | | | | | | |

Place an "X" in one box in each row so that no condition is contradicted.

# The Murderer in the Hotel

| Statements | | Association | | |
|---|---|---|---|---|
| false | hyp. | 1-dim. | 2-dim. | Math. |
| | ✔ | | ✔ | |

SOLUTION SCHEME

Make a chart for yourself as follows:

| | is the murderer | is the victim |
|---|---|---|
| Arlene | | |
| Brenda | | |
| Cheryl | | |
| Daniel | | |
| Emmett | | |
| Farley | | |

Place an "X" in one box in each column so that no condition is contradicted.

# The Three Groups

Anita, Beryl, and Chloe live on an island inhabited by three groups: the Trusties, the Fibbers, and the Normals.

[1] Each is either a Trusty who always tells the truth, a Fibber who always lies, or a Normal who may do either.

[2] Anita says: "If we are all from the same group, then that group is the Fibbers."

[3] Beryl says: "If just one of us belongs to a different group from each of the others, then that one is a Fibber."

[4] Chloe says: "If each of us belongs to a different group from each of the others, then I am a Fibber."

Whose group do you know?

*Classification and Solution
Scheme, page 42;
Solution, page 95.*

# Code Word

S L I D E

− D E A N

―――――――

3 6 5 1

Each of seven digits from 0, 1, 2, 3, 4, 5, 6, 7, 8, and 9 is represented by a different letter in the subtraction problem above.

What word represents 3 6 5 1?

*Classification and Solution
Scheme, page 43;
Solution, page 96.*

# The Three Groups

CLASSIFICATION

| Statements | | Association | | |
|---|---|---|---|---|
| false | hyp. | 1-dim. | 2-dim. | Math. |
| ✔ | ✔ | | | |

SOLUTION SCHEME

Make a chart for yourself as follows:

| Anita | Beryl | Chloe |
|---|---|---|
| | | |
| | | |
| | | |
| | | |
| | | |

Write "Trusty," "Fibber," or "Normal" in each box in as many ways as possible—crossing off any unused boxes—so that no condition is contradicted.

# Code Word

| Statements | | Association | | |
|---|---|---|---|---|
| false | hyp. | 1-dim. | 2-dim. | Math. |
| | | | | ✔ |

*SOLUTION SCHEME*

Make a chart for yourself as follows:

| □ | □ | □ | □ | □ |
|---|---|---|---|---|

| − | □ | □ | □ | □ |
|---|---|---|---|---|
| | 3 | 6 | 5 | 1 |

Write a digit in each box—to discover its corresponding letter—so that the one condition is not contradicted.

# The Winning Mark

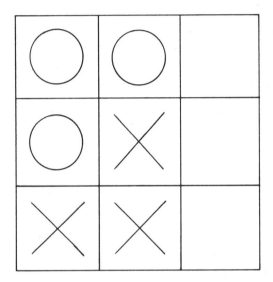

The game of tic-tac-toe is played in a large square divided into nine small squares.

[1] Each of two players in turn places his or her mark—usually X or O—in a small square.

[2] The player who first gets three marks in a horizontal, vertical, or diagonal line wins.

[3] A player will always place his or her mark in a line that already contains (a) two of his or her own marks or (b) two of his or her opponent's marks—giving (a) priority over (b).

Only the last mark to be placed in the game shown above is not given.

Which mark—X or O—wins the game?

*Classification and Solution Scheme, page 46; Solution, page 97.*

# A Big Party

Someone is heard to say truthfully:

[1] "At the party there were
       14 adults,
       17 children,
       12 males, and
       19 females.

[2] Then I arrived and the number of different man-woman couples possible became equal to the number of different boy-girl couples possible. ( If there were 6 men and 8 women at the party, then there would have been 6 × 8 or 48 man-woman couples possible. )"

Is the speaker a man, woman, a boy, or a girl?

*Classification and Solution Scheme, page 47; Solution, page 98.*

# The Winning Mark

*CLASSIFICATION*

| Statements | | Association | | |
|---|---|---|---|---|
| false | hyp. | 1-dim. | 2-dim. | Math. |
| | | ✔ | ✔ | |

*SOLUTION SCHEME*

Make a diagram for yourself as follows:

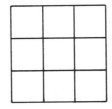

Write "fifth" or "sixth" in each of two small squares in the diagram (to indicate the order in which the marks were placed in the diagram) so that no condition is contradicted.

# A Big Party

*CLASSIFICATION*

| Statements | | Association | | |
|---|---|---|---|---|
| false | hyp. | 1-dim. | 2-dim. | Math. |
| | | | | ✔ |

*SOLUTION SCHEME*

Make a chart for yourself as follows:

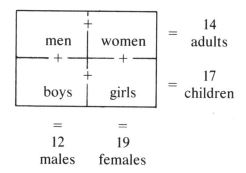

Write a number in each box so that [2] is not contradicted.

# The Tennis Game

Four people are about to play a tennis game.

[1] The four people are Mr. and Mrs. Jones and Mr. and Mrs. Smith.

[2] The worst player is directly across the net from the better Jones player.

[3] The better male player is diagonally across the net from the poorer Smith player.

[4] The poorer male and the better female player are on the same side of the net.

Who is the best player?

*Classification and Solution Scheme, page 50; Solution, page 101.*

# Multiples of 7

When completed, this cross-number puzzle has:

[1] Exactly one digit—0, 1, 2, 3, 4, 5, 6, 7, 8, or 9—in each hexagonal box.

[2] Only numbers that are multiples of seven (0×7, 1×7, 2×7, etc.) when read down and diagonally downward toward the right and left (BE, ADG, CF; AC, BDF, EG; AB, CDE, FG).

[3] No two numbers the same.

What number does ADG represent?

*Classification and Solution Scheme, page 51; Solution, page 102.*

# The Tennis Game

*SOLUTION SCHEME*

Make a diagram for yourself as follows:

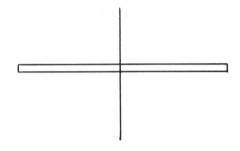

Write "Mr. Jones," "Mrs. Jones," "Mr. Smith," or "Mrs. Smith" in each of the four parts of the tennis-court diagram and write "worst," "better Jones," "better male," "poorer Smith," "poorer male," or "better female" in each of the four parts so that no condition is contradicted.

# Multiples of 7

*CLASSIFICATION*

| Statements | | Association | | |
|---|---|---|---|---|
| false | hyp. | 1-dim. | 2-dim. | Math. |
| | | | ✔ | ✔ |

*SOLUTION SCHEME*

Make a diagram for yourself as follows:

Write a digit (0, 1, 2, 3, 4, 5, 6, 7, 8, 9) in each box so that no one condition is contradicted.

# Harry Will Marry

Harry will marry April, Bette, or Clare.

[1] Of April and Bette:
  (a) Either both have hazel eyes or both do not.
  (b) One is red-haired and the other is not.

[2] Of April and Clare:
  (a) Either both are red-haired or both are not.
  (b) One is slender and the other is not.

[3] Of Bette and Clare:
  (a) One has hazel eyes and the other does not.
  (b) One is slender and the other is not.

[4] Of the mentioned characteristics—hazel eyes, red-haired, and slender:
  (a) If any of April, Bette, and Clare has exactly two of these characteristics, then Harry will marry only the woman with the least number of them.
  (b) If any of April, Bette, and Clare has exactly one of these characteristics, then Harry will marry only the woman with the greatest number of them.

Who will Harry marry?

*Classification and Solution Scheme, page 54; Solution, page 104.*

# The President

Aubrey, Blaine, and Curtis live on an island inhabited by three groups: the Truthtellers, the Falsifiers, and the Alternators.

[1] Each is either a Truthteller who always tells the truth, a Falsifier who always lies, or an Alternator who alternately tells the truth and lies.

[2] One of the three is President of the island.

[3] Aubrey says: (a) "The President belongs to a different group from each of the other two of us."
(b) "Blaine is not the President."

[4] Blaine says: (a) "The President is a Falsifier."
(b) "Aubrey is not the President."

[5] Curtis says: (a) "Exactly two of us belong to the same group."
(b) "I am not the President."

Who is the President?

*Classification and Solution Scheme, page 55;
Solution, page 105.*

# Harry Will Marry

| Statements | | Association | | |
|---|---|---|---|---|
| false | hyp. | 1-dim. | 2-dim. | Math. |
| | ✔ | | | |

*SOLUTION SCHEME*

Make a chart for yourself as follows:

| | Is April | Is Bette | Is Clare |
|---|---|---|---|
| hazel-eyed? | | | |
| red-haired? | | | |
| slender? | | | |

Write "yes" or "no" in each box so that no condition is contradicted.

# The President

*CLASSIFICATION*

| Statements | | Association | | |
|---|---|---|---|---|
| false | hyp. | 1-dim. | 2-dim. | Math. |
| ✔ | | | | |

*SOLUTION SCHEME*

Make a chart for yourself as follows:

| | is true | is false |
|---|---|---|
| [3a] | | |
| [3b] | | |
| [4a] | | |
| [4b] | | |
| [5a] | | |
| [5b] | | |

Place an "X" in one box in each row so that no condition is contradicted.

# Apartments

Avery, Blake, Clark, and Doyle each live in an apartment.

[1] Their apartments are arranged like this:

| a | b | c | d |
|---|---|---|---|

→ East

[2] One of the four is the landlord.

[3] If Clark's apartment is not next to Blake's apartment, then the landlord is Avery and lives in apartment a.

[4] If Avery's apartment is east of Clark's apartment, then the landlord is Doyle and lives in apartment d.

[5] If Blake's apartment is not next to Doyle's apartment, then the landlord is Clark and lives in apartment c.

[6] If Doyle's apartment is east of Avery's apartment, then the landlord is Blake and lives in apartment b.

Who is the landlord?

*Classification and Solution Scheme, page 58; Solution, page 106.*

# Murderer's Occupation

In attempting to solve a murder, six detectives each arrived at a different one of the following descriptions of the murderer.

| | Occupation | Sex | Height in inches | Weight in pounds | Age in years | Smoker |
|---|---|---|---|---|---|---|
| [1] | author | male | 63 to 66 | 110 to 130 | 20 to 30 | cigarette |
| [2] | barber | female | 66 to 69 | 130 to 150 | 30 to 40 | cigar |
| [3] | cooper | male | 69 to 72 | 130 to 150 | 20 to 30 | pipe |
| [4] | draper | male | 63 to 66 | 150 to 170 | 40 to 50 | cigar |
| [5] | editor | female | 63 to 66 | 170 to 190 | 20 to 30 | cigarette |
| [6] | farmer | female | 72 to 75 | 110 to 130 | 50 to 60 | non- |

It turned out that:

[7] Each detective was correct in the same number of the six listed particulars as any other detective.

[8] Exactly one of each kind of particular was correct.

What was the occupation of the murderer?

*Classification and Solution Scheme, page 59; Solution, page 107.*

# Apartments

*CLASSIFICATION*

| Statements | | Association | | |
|---|---|---|---|---|
| false | hyp. | 1-dim. | 2-dim. | Math. |
| | ✔ | ✔ | | |

*SOLUTION SCHEME*

Make a diagram for yourself as follows:

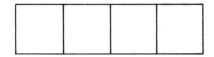

Write "Avery," "Blake," "Clark," or "Doyle" in each box so that no condition is contradicted.

# Murderer's Occupation

*CLASSIFICATION*

| Statements | | Association | | |
|---|---|---|---|---|
| false | hyp. | 1-dim. | 2-dim. | Math. |
| ✔ | | | | ✔ |

*SOLUTION SCHEME*

Make a chart for yourself as follows:

| Occupation | Sex | Height in inches | Weight in pounds | Age in years | Smoker |
|---|---|---|---|---|---|
| author | male | 63 to 66 | 110 to 130 | 20 to 30 | cigarette |
| barber | female | 66 to 69 | 130 to 150 | 30 to 40 | cigar |
| cooper | male | 69 to 72 | 130 to 150 | 20 to 30 | pipe |
| draper | male | 63 to 66 | 150 to 170 | 40 to 50 | cigar |
| editor | female | 63 to 66 | 170 to 190 | 20 to 30 | cigarette |
| farmer | female | 72 to 75 | 110 to 130 | 50 to 60 | non- |

Cross off entries in the boxes (to indicate incorrect information) so that neither [7] nor [8] is contradicted.

# The Owner of the Table

Six people were seated around a table.

[1] Their chairs were arranged around the rectangular table like this:

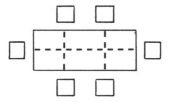

[2] The six people were three women—Althea, Blythe, and Cecile—and three men—Dudley, Edward, and Foster.

[3] Althea sat opposite Blythe or Dudley.

[4] Edward sat to the immediate left of Cecile.

[5] Foster sat to the immediate left of one woman and to the immediate right of another woman.

[6] The person who owned the table was the only person who sat both opposite a man and to the left of a woman.

Who owned the table?

*Classification and Solution Scheme, page 62; Solution, page 109.*

# Family Murder

Statement I. I am the mother of the murderer, but not the mother of the victim.

Statement II. I am the mother of the victim, but not the mother of the murderer.

Statement III. I am the same sex as the victim.

Of the statements above and the people who made them:

[1] Each statement was made by a different one of four people—Alice, her mother, her brother (her mother's son), and her son.

[2] The one person of these four who made no statement is the victim, murdered by one of the other three.

[3] Exactly one of the three statements is false.

Who is the murderer?

*Classification and Solution Scheme, page 63; Solution, page 110.*

# The Owner of the Table

*SOLUTION SCHEME*

Make a diagram for yourself as follows:

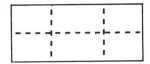

Using the symbols A for Althea, B for Blythe, C for Cecile, D for Dudley, E for Edward, and F for Foster, place the people around the table so that no condition is contradicted.

# Family Murder

CLASSIFICATION

| Statements | | Association | | |
|---|---|---|---|---|
| false | hyp. | 1-dim. | 2-dim. | Math. |
| ✔ | | | ✔ | |

*SOLUTION SCHEME*

Make a chart for yourself as follows:

| | made Statement I | made Statement II | made Statement III | made the false statement |
|---|---|---|---|---|
| Alice | | | | |
| Her mother | | | | |
| Her brother | | | | |
| Her son | | | | |
| The murderer | | | | |

Place an "X" in each of five boxes so that no condition is contradicted.

# The Dart Game

Three men—Arnold, Buford, and Conrad—played a dart game.

[1] Each dart that lodged in the game board scored 1, 5, 10, 25, 50, or 100 points.

[2] Each man threw nine darts that lodged in the board.

[3] Each man's total score was the same as any other man's total score.

[4] No number of points scored by a dart was scored by more than one man.

[5] Arnold scored all the 5s and Buford scored all the 10s.

Who scored all the 100s?

*Classification and Solution*
*Scheme, page 66;*
*Solution, page 112.*

# Hotel Rooms

Six people stayed at a hotel.

[1] The six people were three men—Arden, Brian, and Clyde—and three women.

[2] Each stayed in a different one of six rooms arranged like this:

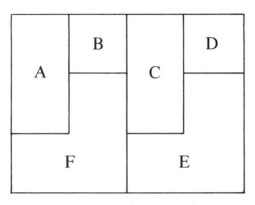

[3] Arden said: "I stayed in a large room."

[4] Brian said: "I stayed in a medium-sized room."

[5] Clyde said: "I stayed in a small room."

[6] Exactly one man lied.

[7] Of the three rooms occupied by the men, only the room occupied by the man who lied bordered on exactly two of the rooms occupied by the women.

Who lied?

*Classification and Solution Scheme, page 67; Solution, page 113.*

# The Dart Game

| Statements | | Association | | |
|---|---|---|---|---|
| false | hyp. | 1-dim. | 2-dim. | Math. |
| | | | | ✔ |

*SOLUTION SCHEME*

Make a chart for yourself as follows:

| | 1s | 5s | 10s | 25s | 50s | 100s | scored this total number of points |
|---|---|---|---|---|---|---|---|
| | | scored this number of | | | | | |
| Arnold | | | | | | | |
| Buford | | | | | | | |
| Conrad | | | | | | | |

Write a number in each box so that no condition is contradicted.

# Hotel Rooms

| Statements | | Association | | |
|---|---|---|---|---|
| false | hyp. | 1-dim. | 2-dim. | Math. |
| ✔ | | | ✔ | |

*SOLUTION SCHEME*

Make a diagram for yourself as follows:

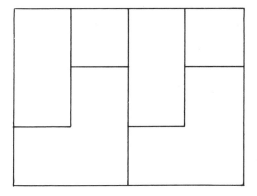

Write "Arden," "Brian," or "Clyde" in each of three parts of the diagram and write "woman" in each of the remaining three parts so that no condition is contradicted.

# The Numbered Discs

Three women were seated around a table.

[1] After the three women were blindfolded, a numbered disc was pasted on each of their foreheads.

[2] The women were then truthfully told "Each of you has either a 1, a 2, or a 3 on your forehead, and the sum of your numbers is either 6 or 7."

[3] After the blindfolds were removed, each woman in turn was asked to name the number on her forehead without seeing it.

[4] The question was repeated until only one woman failed to name the number on her forehead.

[5] When it was logically possible to name the number on her forehead, each woman did so; when it was not logically possible to name the number on her forehead, each woman said "I do not know the number" and waited until the question was repeated to her next time around.

[6] Each of the three women had a 2 on her forehead.

Which woman failed to name her number: the first woman asked, the second woman asked, or the third woman asked?

*Classification and Hint, page 70;*
*Solution, page 114.*

# Finishing First

Here are various predictions on the order in which some entrants in a race would finish, together with a summary of how correct each prediction was.

|     | \| Predictions on the entrant finishing | | | | | \| Number of entrants finishing in first through fifth positions that were predicted in the | |
| --- | --- | --- | --- | --- | --- | --- | --- |
|     | first | second | third | fourth | fifth | right position | wrong position |
| [1] | Ada | Bea | Cal | Don | Eve | 2 | 1 |
| [2] | Flo | Guy | Hal | Eve | Don | 0 | 1 |
| [3] | Guy | Cal | Eve | Ida | Jan | 0 | 2 |
| [4] | Flo | Guy | Ken | Bea | Ida | 1 | 2 |
| [5] | Guy | Flo | Eve | Ada | Cal | 1 | 1 |

Who finished first in the race?

*Classification and Solution Scheme, page 71;*
*Solution, page 116.*

# The Numbered Discs

CLASSIFICATION

| Statements | | Association | | |
|---|---|---|---|---|
| false | hyp. | 1-dim. | 2-dim. | Math. |
| | | ✔ | | ✔ |

*HINT*

Assume the women are questioned in a clockwise order. Then the woman at the →, who is the woman clockwise to the woman at the ?, knows the woman at the ? sees either:

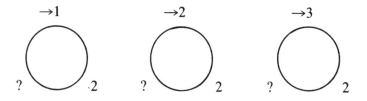

# Finishing First

| Statements | | Association | | |
|---|---|---|---|---|
| false | hyp. | 1-dim. | 2-dim. | Math. |
| ✔ | | ✔ | | ✔ |

*SOLUTION SCHEME*

Make a chart for yourself as follows:

| First | Second | Third | Fourth | Fifth |
|---|---|---|---|---|
| | | | | |

Write "Ada," "Bea," "Cal," "Don," "Eve," "Flo," "Guy," "Hal," "Ida," "Jan," or "Ken" in each box so that no condition is contradicted.

# The Lead in the Play

Five adults were in a play.

[1] The five adults were Tyrone, his sister, their mother, his son, and his daughter.

[2] Each adult had a different one of five dressing rooms arranged like this:

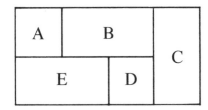

[3] The dressing room of the lead in the play and the dressing room of the lead's sibling bordered on the same number of rooms.

[4] The dressing room of the lead and the dressing room of the lead's parent were the same size.

[5] Tyrone's dressing room did not border on his daughter's dressing room.

[6] Everyone's dressing room bordered on at least one man's dressing room and one woman's dressing room.

Who was the lead?

*Classification and Solution
Scheme, page 74.
Solution, page 117.*

# The Center Card

There are nine cards.

[1] The cards are arranged like this:

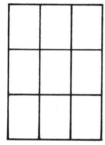

[2] Every ace borders on a king and on a queen.

[3] Every king borders on a queen and on a jack.

[4] Every queen borders on a jack.

[5] There are at least two aces, two kings, two queens, and two jacks.

What kind of card is in the center?

*Classification and Solution
Scheme, page 75;
Solution, page 118.*

# The Lead in the Play

| Statements | | Association | | |
| --- | --- | --- | --- | --- |
| false | hyp. | 1-dim. | 2-dim. | Math. |
| | | | ✓✓ | |

*SOLUTION SCHEME*

Make a diagram for yourself as follows:

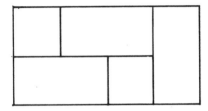

Write "Tyrone," "his sister," "their mother," "his son," or "his daughter" in each of the five parts of the diagram so that no condition is contradicted.

# The Center Card

*CLASSIFICATION*

| Statements | | Association | | |
|---|---|---|---|---|
| false | hyp. | 1-dim. | 2-dim. | Math. |
| | | | ✔ | |

*SOLUTION SCHEME*

Make a diagram for yourself as follows:

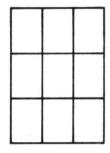

Write "ace," "king," "queen," or "jack" in each part of the diagram so that no condition is contradicted.

# Dogs and Cats

Angus, Basil, Craig, and Duane have pets.

[1] Angus says: "If Duane and I each have a dog, then exactly one of Basil and Craig has a dog."

[2] Basil says: "If Craig and I each have a cat, then exactly one of Angus and Duane has a dog."

[3] Craig says: "If Angus and I each have a dog, then exactly one of Basil and Duane has a cat."

[4] Duane says: "If Basil and I each have a cat, then exactly one of Basil and I has a dog."

[5] Only one of the four is telling the truth.

Who is telling the truth?

*Classification and Solution Scheme, page 78; Solution, page 120*

# The Omitted Age

When completed, this cross-number puzzle

[1] Has exactly one digit—0, 1, 2, 3, 4, 5, 6, 7, 8, or 9—in each box.

[2] Has no zero in a box that contains a, b, c, or d.

| | a | b |
|---|---|---|
| c | | |
| d | | |

[3] Has these definitions:

### ACROSS

a. Abigail's age

c. Sum of Abigail's age, Blanche's age, Cynthia's age, and Darlene's age

d. Blanche's age

### DOWN

a. Sum of three of the ages in c across

b. Cynthia's age.

c. Darlene's age

Whose age was omitted from a down?

*Classification and Solution Scheme, page 79; Solution, page 121.*

# Dogs and Cats

| Statements | | Association | | |
|---|---|---|---|---|
| false | hyp. | 1-dim. | 2-dim. | Math. |
| ✔ | ✔ | | | |

*SOLUTION SCHEME*

Make a chart for yourself as follows:

| | Does Angus | Does Basil | Does Craig | Does Duane |
|---|---|---|---|---|
| have a dog? | | | | |
| have a cat? | | | | |

Write "yes" or "no" in each box so that no condition is contradicted.

# The Omitted Age

*CLASSIFICATION*

| Statements | | Association | | |
|---|---|---|---|---|
| false | hyp. | 1-dim. | 2-dim. | Math. |
| | | | ✔ | ✔ |

*SOLUTION SCHEME*

Make a diagram and charts for yourself as follows:

Write "A," "B," "C," "D," "E," "F," or "G" in each box of the charts so that no condition is contradicted and so that no addition is impossible.

# The Hats

Four men were seated around a table.

[1] After the four men were blindfolded, a colored hat was placed on each of their heads.

[2] The men were then truthfully told: "The hat on each of your heads was chosen from among two white hats, two black hats, and one red hat."

[3] After the fifth hat was taken away, the blindfolds were removed and each man in turn was asked to name the color of the hat on his head without seeing it.

[4] The question was repeated until only one man failed to name the color of the hat on his head.

[5] When it was logically possible to name the color of the hat on his head, each man did so; when it was not logically possible to name the color of the hat on his head, each man said "I do not know the color" and waited until the question was repeated to him the next time around.

[6] None of the four men received the red hat.

Which man failed to name the color of his hat: the first man asked, the second man asked, the third man asked, or the fourth man asked?

*Classification and Hint,*
*page 83;*
*Solution, page 123.*

# The Dart Board

Three women—Alma, Bess, and Cleo—played a dart game.

[1] Here is the dart board they used:

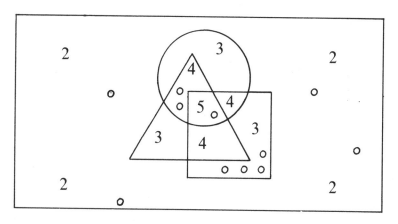

[a] Where a player's dart lodged in the board is indicated by o.

[b] The number of points scored by a dart, when it lodged in one of the various regions on the board, is indicated by 2, 3, 4, or 5.

[2] Each woman's total score was the same as any other woman's total score.

[3] Alma said: "If I was the first to score in the square, then I scored at least one 2."

[4] Bess said: "If I was the first to score in the triangle, then Alma and Cleo did not score the same number of 2s."

[5] Cleo said: "If I was the first to score in the circle, then I did not score more 2s than Bess."

[6] Only one woman told the truth.

Who scored the 5?

*Classification and Solution Scheme, page 84; Solution, page 126.*

# The Hats

| Statements | | Association | | |
|---|---|---|---|---|
| false | hyp. | 1-dim. | 2-dim. | Math. |
| | | ✔ | | |

*HINT*

Let X represent one color hat of two black hats and two white hats, and let Y represent the other color hat; let R represent a red hat. Assume the men are questioned in a clockwise order. Then the man at the →, who is the man clockwise to the man at the ?, knows the man at the ? sees either:

| Case a | Case b | Case c |
|---|---|---|

**83**

# The Dart Board

| Statements | | Association | | |
|---|---|---|---|---|
| false | hyp. | 1-dim. | 2-dim. | Math. |
| ✔ | ✔ | ✔ | ✔ | ✔ |

*SOLUTION SCHEME*

Make a chart for yourself as follows:

| | scored this number of | | | | scored this total number of points |
|---|---|---|---|---|---|
| | 2s | 3s | 4s | 5s | |
| Alma | | | | | |
| Bess | | | | | |
| Cleo | | | | | |

Write a number in each box so that no condition is contradicted.

# Solutions

# Vera's Preference

From [1]: (I) exactly one of Adam, Boyd, Cary, and Dirk has none of the preferred traits; (II) exactly one of Adam, Boyd, Cary, and Dirk has all of the preferred traits.

So, from [4] and [5]: either (x) Adam and Cary are both tall and Boyd and Dirk are both fair; or (y) Adam and Cary are both short and Boyd and Dirk are both dark. From [2], y is impossible; so x is the correct situation.

Then, from [3], Boyd is short and handsome. Then, from I, Dirk is short and unhandsome. Then, from [2]), Adam is fair. Then, from II, Cary is dark and handsome. So, *Cary is tall, dark, and handsome.*

Then, from [1], Adam is handsome.

# Speaking of Tennis

From [2] and [3]:

| speaker | speaker's partner |
|---|---|
| | |
| server's daughter | receiver's father |

| speaker | speaker's partner server |
|---|---|
| | |
| server's daughter receiver | receiver's father |

Then, from [4], either:

Case I

| speaker<br>receiver | speaker's partner |
| --- | --- |
| server's daughter | receiver's father<br>server |

Case II

Then, in Case II, the receiver's father/server was the father of both the receiver and the server's daughter. From [1], this situation is impossible. So Case II is not a correct case.

Then Case I is a correct case. Then the server's daughter/receiver was the daughter of both the server and the receiver's father. So, from [1], the server's daughter/receiver was Winifred's daughter, the receiver's father was Winifred's husband, and the server was Winifred. Then, from [1], Winifred's father was the fourth player, the speaker. So *Winifred's father spoke.*

Note: If the speaker is placed in the upper right instead of the upper left of the diagram, then the placement of the players will be

| speaker's partner<br>server | speaker |
| --- | --- |
| receiver's father | server's daughter<br>receiver |

but the corresponding identities of the players remain the same.

# Getting Married

Suppose Aaron got married. Then, from [1] and [4], Aaron married Olive. But this situation is impossible, from [1] and [5].

Suppose Colin got married. Then, from [1] and [3], Colin married Norma. But this situation is impossible, from [1] and [2].

Suppose David got married. Then, from [3] and [4], David married Norma and Olive. But this situation is impossible, from [1].

So, from [1], Barry got married.

From [1] and [2], Barry did not marry Norma. From [1] and [5], Barry did not marry Olive. From [1] and [2] or from [1] and [5], Barry did not marry Pearl.

So, from [1], *Barry and Marie got married.*

# My House Number

Suppose my house number is a multiple of 3. Then, from [1], it is either 51, 54, or 57. But, from [2], it cannot be any of these numbers because none is a multiple of 4. So my house number is not a multiple of 3.

Then my house number is not a multiple of 6 because a multiple of 6 is a multiple of 3. So, from [3], it is a number from 70 through 79. Then, because it is not a multiple of 3, it is either 70, 71, 73, 74, 76, 77, or 79.

Then, from [2], it cannot be "not a multiple of 4," so it *is* a multiple of 4. Then *my house number is 76*, because it is either 70, 71, 73, 74, 76, 77, or 79, and of these only 76 is a multiple of 4.

# The Murderer in the Mansion

From [2] and [3], the detective arrived at midnight and at least one of the three visitors arrived after midnight. Then, from [4], Crain arrived after midnight. So Crain was not the detective. Then, from [4] and [5], Bixby was not the detective. So, from [2], Allen was the detective. Then, from [6],

Crain was not the murderer. Then, from [1] and [4], Allen arrived after Bixby and *Allen was the murderer.*

In summary: Bixby arrived before midnight; Allen, who was both detective and murderer, arrived at midnight; and Crain arrived after midnight.

## The Cube

Either S occurs twice or S occurs once on the cube. If S occurs twice on the cube: then, from [2],

then, from [1],  and H would have to be on the

face where E is. This situation is impossible.

So S occurs once on the cube. Then, from [2],

; then, from [3], ; then, from [1],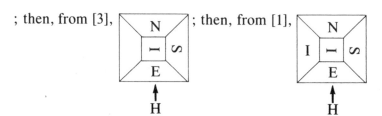

So *I occurs twice on the cube.*

# Three-Letter Word

From [1] and [2], none of the three logicians was told the word had an N; otherwise a logician would know that the word had one vowel. So the word is not INN or PEN.

Then, from [1] and [3], none of the three logicians was told the word had an I; otherwise a logician would know the word, now one of four, had two vowels. So the word is not PIE or TIE.

Then, from [1] and [4], the logician who knows the word must have been told a letter that is in only one of the two remaining words, PET and TEE. So that logician was told the word had a P and *the word is PET*.

# Esther's Fiancé

From [2] and [6]: If Esther always tells the truth, then her fiancé always tells the truth; if Esther always lies, then her fiancé always tells the truth. So Esther's fiancé always tells the truth.

Then, from [1] and [2]: If the declaration in [5] is false, then Claude lied and Dexter is the truth-telling fiancé. Then the declaration in [3] is false. Then the declaration in [4] is false. Then the declaration in [3] is true. Because the declaration in [3] is both false and true, this situation is impossible. So the declaration in [5] is true.

Then, from a true declaration in [5], the declaration in [3] is false. Then, because Esther's fiancé always tells the truth, *Barton is Esther's fiancé*. Then the declaration in [4] is true. Then Dexter always tells the truth.

Esther's declaration in [6] may be either true or false.

# Family Occupations

From [2] and [4], the singer and the dancer are not both men. From [4] and [5], if the singer is a man, then the dancer must be a man. So the singer is a woman and either:

|         | Singer is a | Dancer is a |
|---------|-------------|-------------|
| Case I  | woman       | woman       |
| Case II | woman       | man         |

Suppose Case I is true. Then, from [1] and [2], the dancer is Mr. Brown's wife and the singer is Mr. Brown's daughter.

Suppose Case II is true. Then, from [1], [3], and [5], the singer and the dancer are neither Mr. Brown's wife and Mr. Brown, respectively, nor Mr. Brown's daughter and Mr. Brown's son, respectively. Then, from [1] and [5], the dancer is Mr. Brown and the singer is Mr. Brown's daughter.

So, in either case, you know *Mr. Brown's daughter is the singer.*

# A Small Party

Suppose [4] through [6] are all true. Then [1] is false, and [2] and [3] cannot both be true. From [7], this situation is impossible.

So, from [7], one of [4] through [6] is false, and [1] through [3] are all true. Then, from [1] and [2], there were 11 men and women. Then, from [3], either: (A) there were 8 men and 3 women; or (B) there were 3 men and 8 women.

Suppose A is correct. Then, from [2], there was 1 child. Then [4] and [5] are both false, contradicting [7]. So A is not correct.

Then B is correct. Then, from [2], there were 6 children. Then *[4] is false*.


# The Separated Couple

From [1] and [2], either ($W_A$ is Alden woman, M is man, and $M_B$ is Brent man):

Then the man sitting across from Mrs. Alden was not Mr. Drake, from [3], and was not Mr. Alden, from [4]. So the man sitting across from Mrs. Alden was Mr. Crown.

Then, from [3], the man who sat on Mrs. Crown's immediate left was Mr. Alden and, from [3], Mrs. Crown could not have sat in chair h in Case I, nor in chair a or f in Case II. From [4], Mrs. Crown could not have sat in chair b, c, or d in Case I, nor in chair c or g in Case II. So Mrs. Crown sat either in chair g in Case I or in chair h in Case II. So, from [3] and [4], either ($W_C$ is Crown woman, $M_A$ is Alden man, $M_C$ is Crown man, and $M_D$ is Drake man):

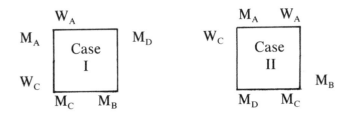

Then, from [4], Case I is impossible because either the Blakes sat next to each other and the Drakes sat next to each other, or the Blakes sat across from each other. So Case II is the correct one. Then *the Crowns did not sit next to each other* and, from [4], Mrs. Brent and Mrs. Drake each sat next to her husband.

## The Opposite Sex

From [2] and [3], Marion cannot be an only daughter and have a sister; so Marion is a male. Then, from [3], Marion is Carmen's brother.

From [2], Marion's sister is either Evelyn or Leslie. Suppose Evelyn is Marion's sister; then, from [1], Carmen is Leslie's only son. But, from previous reasoning, Marion is Carmen's brother; so Marion would also be Leslie's son. This situation contradicts [1]. So Leslie, not Evelyn, is Marion's sister.

Then, from [1], Evelyn is Leslie's only son.

It is now known that Marion and Evelyn are males and Leslie is a female. So, from [4], *Leslie is the opposite sex from each of the others* and Carmen is a male.

In summary: Leslie is a female, Marion and Carmen are her brothers, and Evelyn is her son.

## Truth Day

From [1], Philip's declarations in [3] and [5] cannot both be false; otherwise he tells the truth on more than one of the days of the week. From [1] and the fact that the declarations in [3] through [5] were made on consecutive days, Philip's declarations in [3] and [5] cannot both be true; otherwise he tells the truth on more than one of the days of the week. So either Philip's declaration in [3] is the only true one or his declaration in [5] is the only true one.

Suppose his declaration in [3] is the only true one. Then, from his false declaration in [5], he made the declaration in [3] on a Wednesday or a Friday. Then, from [2], his false declaration in [4] was made on a Thursday or a Saturday. This situation is impossible.

So his declaration in [5] is the only true one. Then, from his false declaration in [3], he made the declaration in [5] on a Monday or a Tuesday. Then, from [2], his false declaration in [4] was made on a Sunday or a Monday. His declaration in [4] could not have been made on a Sunday; otherwise his declaration in [4] would be true. So his declaration in [4] was made on a Monday.

Then, from [2], his true declaration in [5] was made on a Tuesday and *Philip tells the truth on Tuesday.*

# The Murderer in the Hotel

From [2], there was only one murderer. So either one hypothesis of [4] and [5] is false or both hypotheses in [4] and [5] are false.

Case I. Suppose both hypotheses in [4] and [5] are false. Then the murderer and the victim stayed in rooms that bordered on the same number of rooms (from [4]), and that were the same size (from [5]). This situation is impossible, from [1].

Case II. Suppose the hypothesis in [4] is true and the hypothesis in [5] is false. Then the murderer and the victim stayed in rooms that bordered on different numbers of rooms (from [4]), and that were the same size (from [5]). Then, from [1], either: (a) Arlene or Farley was the victim and the other was the murderer, (b) Brenda or Daniel was the victim and the other was the murderer, or (c) Cheryl or

Emmett was the victim and the other was the murderer. From [4], a is impossible and, from [3], b and c are impossible.

Case III. So the hypothesis in [5] is true and the hypothesis in [4] is false. Then the murderer and the victim stayed in rooms that bordered on the same number of rooms (from [4]), and that were different in size (from [5]). Then, from [1], either: (d) Arlene or Daniel was the victim and the other was the murderer, (e) Brenda or Emmett was the victim and the other was the murderer, or (f) Cheryl or Farley was the victim and the other was the murderer. From [5], f is impossible and, from [3], e is impossible. Then d is correct and, from [5], *Daniel was the murderer.* So Arlene was the victim.

# The Three Groups

Exactly two of the three hypotheses in [2], [3], and [4] must be false. So, because a hypothetical statement is true when the hypothesis in it is false, at least two of the declarations in [2], [3], and [4] must be true.

Case I. Only the declaration in [2] is false. Then Anita's hypothesis is true and her conclusion is false. Then, from [1], each person is a Normal.

Case II. Only the declaration in [3] is false. Then Beryl's hypothesis is true and her conclusion is false. Then, from [1], Beryl is a Normal. (If Beryl is a Fibber, then someone else must be a Fibber, which is impossible.) Then either Anita and Chloe are both Trusties, Anita is a Trusty and Chloe is a Normal, or Chloe is a Trusty and Anita is a Normal.

Case III. Only the declaration in [4] is false. Then Chloe's hypothesis is true and her conclusion is false. Then, from

[1], Chloe is a Normal and either Anita or Beryl is a Fibber. This situation is impossible, from [1].

Case IV. The declarations in [2], [3], and [4] are all true. Then, because exactly one of their hypotheses is true, one of their conclusions is true. Then at least one person is a Fibber. This situation is impossible, from [1].

In summary: Anita is a Trusty or a Normal, Beryl is a Normal, and Chloe is a Trusty or a Normal. So *you know Beryl's group.*

## Code Word

S must be 1. Then D (under L) is greater than 5. If D is 6, then L is 0; but then A is 0 or 1, which is impossible. If D is 7, then L is 0 and A is 2. If D is 8, then L is 2; then A is 3. If D is 9, then L is 2 or 3 and A is 3 or 4. So either:

| Case | S | D | L | A |
|------|---|---|---|---|
| i    | 1 | 7 | 0 | 2 |
| ii   | 1 | 8 | 2 | 3 |
| iii  | 1 | 9 | 2 | 3 |
| iv   | 1 | 9 | 2 | 4 |
| v    | 1 | 9 | 3 | 4 |

If 1 was carried from D to E, then N would have to be 9 and D (over A) would have to be 6 more than A. So Case iii is eliminated. Then E (over N) is 1 more than N. So E is not 0.

E is not 1. If E is 2, then N is 1; so E is not 2. If E is 3, then N is 2; so E is not 3.

So E is greater than 3. Then 1 was carried from L to I (or D − L = 6). So Cases i and iv are eliminated.

If E is 4, then N is 3; so E is not 4. If E is 5, then I is 1; so

E is not 5. If E is 7, then I is 3; so E is not 7. If E is 8, then I is 4; so E is not 8. If E is 9, then N is 8; so E is not 9. So E is 6.

Then I is 2 and N is 5. So Case ii is eliminated (because I is 2) and Case v is the correct one.

In summary:

| Case | S | D | L | A | E | I | N |
|------|---|---|---|---|---|---|---|
| v | 1 | 9 | 3 | 4 | 6 | 2 | 5 |

Then *the word that represents 3651 is LENS.*


# The Winning Mark

|   |   |   |
|---|---|---|
| 1 | 2 | 3 |
| 4 | 5 | 6 |
| 7 | 8 | 9 |

Let a number in each square as shown indicate the location of a mark. Then, from [3], the seventh mark must be placed in square 3 where, from [2], it wins for X or 0; or be placed in square 9 where, from [2], it wins for X. So, from [3], the sixth mark must have been placed in a line already containing two of the opponent's marks: either in square 2 or in square 7; otherwise, either X or 0 would have been placed in square 3 or X would have been placed in square 9. So before the sixth mark was placed in a square the situation was either:

Case I          Case II

In Case I an X must be the fifth mark, from [1]. But none of the Xs could be the fifth mark because, from [3], as the fifth mark: the X in square 5 would have been placed in square 9, the X in square 7 would have been placed in square 2, and the X in square 8 would have been placed in square 3. So Case I is not the correct situation.

Then Case II is the correct situation and, from [1], 0 was the fifth mark. Then, from [1], the seventh mark will be 0 and, from [2], *0 wins the game.*

Which 0 was the fifth mark can be determined from [3]. As the fifth mark: the 0 in square 2 would have been placed in square 7 and the 0 in square 4 would have been placed in square 3. So the fifth mark was the 0 in square 1.

# A Big Party

From [1], number number     'So, keeping the spa-

$$\begin{matrix} \text{number} & & \text{number} & \\ \text{of} & + & \text{of} & = 14 \\ \text{men} & & \text{women} & \\ + & & + & \\ \text{number} & & \text{number} & \\ \text{of} & + & \text{of} & = 17 \\ \text{boys} & & \text{girls} & \\ = & & = & \\ 12 & & 19 & \end{matrix}$$

tial relationship indicated, one gets either:

| | | | |
|---|---|---|---|
| 0 + 14 | 1 + 13 | 2 + 12 | 3 + 11 |
| + + | + + | + + | + + |
| 12 + 5, | 11 + 6, | 10 + 7, | 9 + 8, |
| | | | |
| 4 + 10 | 5 + 9 | 6 + 8 | 7 + 7 |
| + + | + | + + | + + |
| 8 + 9, | 7 + 10, | 6 + 11, | 5 + 12, |

$$8 + 6 \qquad 9 + 5 \qquad 10 + 4 \qquad 11 + 3$$
$$+ \quad + \qquad + \quad + \qquad + \quad\ + \qquad + \quad +$$
$$4 + 13, \quad\ 3 + 14, \quad\ 2 + 15, \quad\ 1 + 16,$$

$$\text{or} \quad 12 + 2$$
$$+ \quad +$$
$$0 + 17.$$

Then, from [2], one compares the product of the top two numbers with the product of the bottom two numbers in each case; the difference between the products should be one of the numbers multiplied to get the smaller product. Trial and error reveals that $9 + 5$ is the correct case: $9 \times 5$
$$= 3 \times 14 + 3 \qquad + \quad +$$
$$3 + 14$$

or $9 \times 5 = 3 \times 15$. So *the speaker is a girl.*

This puzzle can also be solved by using algebra, as follows. Let m be the number of male adults. Then, from [1],

$$\text{m} + 14 - \text{m} \qquad = \text{number of adults}$$
$$+ \qquad +$$
$$12 - \text{m} + \text{m} + 5 \qquad = \text{number of children}$$
$$= \qquad =$$
number    number
of males    of females

Then, from [2], the speaker is either a
(I) man: $(m+1) \times (14-m) = (12-m) \times (m+5)$ or (II) woman: $(m) \times (14-m+1) = (12-m) \times (m+5)$ or (III) boy: $(m) \times (14-m) = (12-m+1) \times (m+5)$ or (IV) girl: $(m) \times (14-m) = (12-m) \times (m+5+1)$.

Attempting to solve each equation in turn, one finds that m can be a whole number only in IV:

I. 
$$(m+1) \times (14-m) = (12-m) \times (m+5)$$
$$14m - m + 14 - m^2 = 12m - 5m + 60 - m^2$$
$$13m + 14 = 7m + 60$$
$$6m = 46 \qquad \text{impossible}$$

II. 
$$(m) \times (15-m) = (12-m) \times (m+5)$$
$$15m - m^2 = 12m - 5m + 60 - m^2$$
$$15m = 7m + 60$$
$$8m = 60 \qquad \text{impossible}$$

III. 
$$(m) \times (14-m) = (13-m) \times (m+5)$$
$$14m - m^2 = 13m - 5m + 65 - m^2$$
$$14m = 8m + 65$$
$$6m = 65 \qquad \text{impossible}$$

IV. 
$$(m) \times (14-m) = (12-m) \times (m+6)$$
$$14m - m^2 = 12m - 6m + 72 - m^2$$
$$14m = 6m + 72$$
$$8m = 72$$
$$m = 9$$

So  m + 14 − m  becomes  9 + 5  and *the speaker is a girl.*

$$\begin{array}{cc} + & + \\ 12-m & m+5 \end{array} \qquad \begin{array}{cc} + & + \\ 3 & +14 \end{array}$$

# The Tennis Game

From [3]:   better male | Then, from [2],
─────────────┬─────────────
             │ poorer Smith

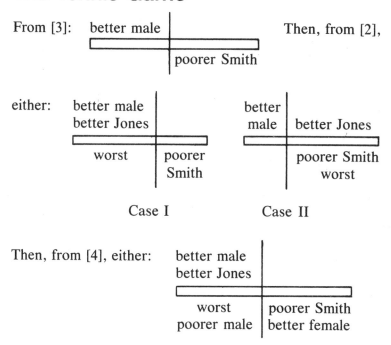

either:   better male | better
          better Jones | male │ better Jones
─────────────┬───────── ──────────┬──────────
    worst   │ poorer           │ poorer Smith
            │ Smith            │ worst

Case I              Case II

Then, from [4], either:   better male
                          better Jones
                      ────────────┬──────────────
                         worst    │ poorer Smith
                       poorer male │ better female

Case I

better male │ better Jones       Then, from [1], either:
─────────────┬─────────────
better female │ poorer Smith
              │   worst
              │ poorer male

Case II

| better male better Jones Mr. Jones | Mrs. Jones |
|---|---|
| worst poorer male Mr. Smith | poorer Smith better female Mrs. Smith |

Case I

| better male Mr. Jones | better Jones Mrs. Jones |
|---|---|
| better female Mrs. Smith | poorer Smith worst poorer male Mr. Smith |

Case II

Then, in Case I, Mr. Smith is the worst player and Mrs. Smith is the poorer Smith player. This situation is impossible. So Case I is not a correct case.

Then Case II is a correct case. Then the worst player is Mr. Smith, the better male player is Mr. Jones, the better Jones player is Mrs. Jones, and the better female player is Mrs. Smith. So *the best player is Mrs. Smith.*

Note: If the better male player is placed in the upper right instead of the upper left of the diagram, then the placement of the players will be

| Mrs. Jones | Mr. Jones |
|---|---|
| Mr. Smith | Mrs. Smith |

; but the

order of playing abilities remains the same.


# Multiples of 7

From [1] and [2], each number represented by AB, AC, BE, CF, EG, and FG is either 00, 07, 14, 21, 28, 35, 42, 49, 56, 63, 70, 77, 84, 91, or 98. Then, from [3] and the listed numbers, A must be either 0, 2, 4, 7, or 9 and G must be either 0, 1, 4, 7, or 8. So:

| | If A is | Then B or C is |
|---|---|---|
| Case I | 0 or 7 | 0 or 7 |
| Case II | 2 or 9 | 1 or 8 |
| Case III | 4 | 2 or 9 |

| Then E or F is | If G is | |
|---|---|---|
| 0 or 7 | 0 or 7 | Case i |
| 2 or 9 | 1 or 8 | Case ii |
| 1 or 8 | 4 | Case iii |

Case I, II, or III must coexist with Case i, ii, or iii so that BE is a multiple of 7.

Case I. If B is 0 or 7, then E must be 0 or 7. Then either 00, 07, 70, or 77 occurs twice among AB, AC, EG, and FG. This situation is impossible, from [3].

Case II. If B is 1 or 8, then E must be 4. This situation is impossible because neither Case i, ii, nor iii allows E to be 4.

Case III. So this case is the correct one. Then B is 2 or 9. Then E is 1 or 8. Then Case iii coexists with Case III.

So A is 4 and G is 4. Then 1 must be carried to G when ADG is divided by 7. So D must be 1 more than 2 which is 3. Then *ADG must represent 434.*

The coexistence of Cases III and iii results in these four possible arrangements of the digits:

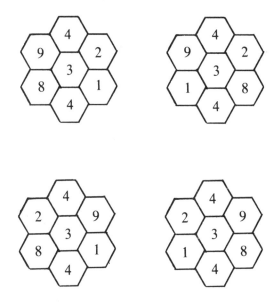

In each arrangement, BDF and CDE are multiples of 7.

# Harry Will Marry

From [1a] and [3a], either (A represents April, B represents Bette, C represents Clare, H represents hazel eyes, h represents no hazel eyes):

| Case I | | | Case II | | |
|---|---|---|---|---|---|
| A | B | C | A | B | C |
| H | H | h | h | h | H |

Then, from [1b] and [2a], either (R represents red hair, r represents no red hair):

| Case Ia | | | Case Ib | | | Case IIa | | | Case IIb | | |
|---|---|---|---|---|---|---|---|---|---|---|---|
| A | B | C | A | B | C | A | B | C | A | B | C |
| H | H | h | H | H | h | h | h | H | h | h | H |
| R | r | R | r | R | r | R | r | R | r | R | r |

From [2b] and [3b], either: (i) Clare is the only one of the three who is slender, or (ii) Clare is the only one of the three who is not slender. From [4], neither i nor ii is possible in Cases Ia and IIb (one woman cannot have exactly one characteristic at the same time that another woman has exactly two characteristics because Harry will marry only one woman). So, from [4], either (S represents slender, s represents not slender):

| Case Ib | | | Case IIa | | |
|---|---|---|---|---|---|
| A | B | C | A | B | C |
| H | H | h | h | h | H |
| r | R | r | R | r | R |
| S | S | s | s | s | S |

Then, from [4a], Harry will marry Clare in Case Ib and, from [4b], Harry will marry Clare in Case IIa. So, in either case, *Harry will marry Clare.*

# The President

Suppose [4a] is true. Then, from [1] and [2], [3b] is true. Then, from [1] and [2], [4b] is true. Then, from [2], Curtis is the President. Then, from [1], [5a] and [5b] are both false. Then, from [1] and because [5a] is false, [3a] is false. But [3a] cannot be false because the President does belong to a different group from each of the other two (from [1]). So [4a] is not true but false.

With [4a] false, suppose [4b] is true and Blaine is the President. Then, because Blaine is the President, [3b] is false and [5b] is true. Then, because Blaine is the President and is an Alternator (from [1]), [3a] is false. Then [5a] can be neither true nor false. So, with [4b] true, Blaine is not the President.

With [4a] false, suppose [4b] is true and Curtis is the President. Then, because Curtis is the President, [3b] is true and [5b] is false. Then, because [4a] and [5b] are false, [5a] is true. Then, because Blaine and Curtis are both Alternators (from [1]) and Curtis is the President, [3a] is false. Then [5a] is false. Then [5a] is both true and false. This situation is impossible. So, with [4b] true, Curtis is not the President.

Then, with [4a] false, [4b] is not true but false. Then, *Aubrey is the President.*

Then [4a] and [4b] are false, and [3b] and [5b] are true. Suppose [3a] is false. Then, because there must be another Alternator along with Aubrey, [5a] is false. But [5a] cannot be false. So [3a] is true. Then, because there must not be another Truthteller, [5a] is false. That [5a] is false is confirmed by the result.

In summary: Aubrey is a Truthteller and the President, Blaine is a Falsifier, and Curtis is an Alternator who first lied and then told the truth.

# Apartments

From [2], there is only one landlord. So no more than one of the conclusions in [3] through [6] is true.

Suppose no conclusion is true in [3] through [6]. Then each hypothesis in [3] through [6] is false. Then, from false hypotheses in [3] and [5], Blake's apartment is between Clark's and Doyle's. Then both hypotheses in [4] and [6] cannot be false. So this situation is impossible.

So exactly one conclusion is true in [3] through [6]. Then, because the other three conclusions are false, the hypotheses associated with the three conclusions are false. Then, because all the hypotheses cannot be false, the hypothesis associated with the true conclusion is true.

Suppose the hypothesis in [3] is the only true hypothesis. Then from [3], Avery lives in apartment a. From [1] and because the hypothesis in [6] is false, this situation is impossible.

Suppose the hypothesis in [4] is the only true hypothesis. Then, from [4], Doyle lives in apartment d. From [1] and because the hypothesis in [6] is false, this situation is impossible.

Suppose the hypothesis in [6] is the only true hypothesis. Then, from [6], Blake lives in apartment b. Then, from [1] and the false hypotheses in [3] and [5], Avery lives in apartment d. From [1] and because the hypothesis in [4] is false, this situation is impossible.

So the hypothesis in [5] is the only true one. Then, from [5], *Clark is the landlord.*

From [5], Clark lives in apartment c. So, from [1] and the false hypotheses in [4] and [6], Blake lives in apartment d. Then, from [1] and the false hypothesis in [6], Doyle lives in apartment a and Avery lives in apartment b. With this arrangement, the hypothesis in [3] is false, as it should be.

# Murderer's Occupation

From [8], as many as fourteen correct choices are possible (only one for occupation, two each for weight and smoking habits, and three each for the other particulars) and as few as eight correct choices are possible (three for sex and one each for the other particulars) in [1] through [6]. From [7], the number of correct choices is a multiple of six. So the number of correct choices is twelve, each detective getting two. The following reasoning uses [1] through [6].

The murderer could not be both 63 to 66 inches tall and 20 to 30 years old; otherwise, one detective would have gotten three particulars correct, including sex. The murderer could not be neither 63 to 66 inches tall nor 20 to 30 years old; otherwise, the number of correct choices would be less than twelve (one for height, one for age, one for occupation, three for sex, and at most two each for weight and smoking habits). So either the murderer is 63 to 66 inches tall or the murderer is 20 to 30 years old, but not both.

Then (because the murderer is either 63 to 66 inches tall or 20 to 30 years old, but not both) two detectives are correct about the weight—110 to 130 pounds or 130 to 150 pounds—and two detectives are correct about the smoking habits—cigarette smoker or cigar smoker; otherwise, the number of correct choices would be less than twelve (four for height and age, one for occupation, three for sex, and less than four for weight and smoking habits).

If the murderer is 63 to 66 inches tall, then the murderer cannot be a male; otherwise, the murderer would be a cigarette smoker or a cigar smoker (already established) and some detective would have more than two correct choices. Then the murderer is a female. Using the fact that each detective got two correct choices, one finds: first, the murderer is a cigar smoker; next, the murderer weighs 110 to 130 pounds; next, no correct age choice is possible. So the murderer is not 63 to 66 inches tall.

Then the murderer is 20 to 30 years old. Then the murderer cannot be a male; otherwise, the murderer would weigh either 110 to 130 pounds or 130 to 150 pounds (already established) and some detective would have more than two correct choices. Then the murderer is a female. Then, from [4], *the murderer is a draper* and a cigar smoker (no other particulars are left in [4]). Then, from [1], the murderer weighs 110 to 130 pounds (no other particular is left in [1]). Then, from [3], the murderer is 69 to 72 inches tall (no other particular is left in [3]).

## The Owner of the Table

From [1] and [6], either ($M_1$ is man, $W_1$ is woman, $\bigcirc$ is owner of table):

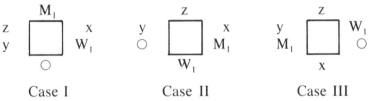

Case I.  Case II.  Case III.

Case I. If x is a man, then y is a man; otherwise z's position contradicts [6]. If x is a woman, then y is a woman; otherwise $W_1$'s position contradicts [6].

Case II. If x is a man, then $\bigcirc$ is a man; otherwise y's position contradicts [6]. If x is a woman, then $\bigcirc$ is a woman; otherwise $M_1$'s position contradicts [6].

Case III. If x is a man, then y is a man; otherwise z's position contradicts [6]. But if x is a man and y is a man, then $W_1$'s position contradicts [6], from [2]. So this situation is impossible. If x is a woman, then $\bigcirc$ is a woman; otherwise $M_1$'s position contradicts [6]. But if x is a woman and $\bigcirc$ is a woman, then x's position contradicts [6], from [2]. So this situation is impossible.

So either ($M_1$ is first man, $M_2$ is second man, etc.):

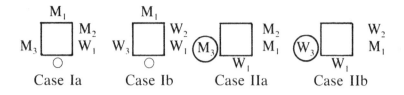

Case Ia    Case Ib    Case IIa    Case IIb

Then, from [2], either:

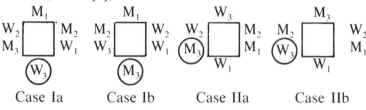

Case Ia    Case Ib    Case IIa    Case IIb

Then, from [5] followed by [4] followed by [2], either ($W_C$ is Cecile, $M_D$ is Dudley, $M_E$ is Edward, and $M_F$ is Foster):

Case Ia    Case Ib    Case IIa    Case IIb

Then, from [3], Cases Ia, Ib, and IIa are impossible and Case IIb is correct. Then *Cecile owned the table*. From [3], $W_1$ is Althea; then, from [2], $W_2$ is Blythe.

# Family Murder

Suppose Statements I and II are both true. Then, from [1], a different woman made each one. Then, from [1], a man made Statement III. Then, from [1] and [2], the victim is a man. Then Statement III is true. This situation contradicts [3], so it is impossible. Then, from [3], either Statement I or Statement II is false and Statement III is true.

Suppose the true Statement III was made by a woman. Then, from [1] and [2], Statements I and II were each made by a different man. Then both Statements I and II are false. This situation contradicts [3], so it is impossible. Then the true Statement III was made by a man. Then the victim was a man. Then, from [1] and [2], one of Statements I and II was made by Alice and the other was made by Alice's mother; and either Alice's brother or Alice's son is the victim.

Suppose Statement II is the false statement. (A) If Alice's brother is the victim, Alice's mother could not have made a true Statement I; so Alice's mother made a false Statement II and Alice is the murderer. But then Alice would have to have made a true Statement I. This situation is impossible. (B) If Alice's son is the victim, Alice could not have made a true Statement I; so Alice made a false Statement II and Alice's son is the murderer. This situation is impossible. So, from A and B, Statement II is not the false statement.

Then, from [3], Statement I is the false statement. (C) If Alice's brother is the victim, Alice's mother made a true Statement II. Then Alice is not the murderer and Alice made a false Statement I. Then Alice's son is not the murderer. Then Alice's mother is the murderer. (D) If Alice's son is the victim, Alice made a true Statement II. Then Alice's mother made a false Statement I. Then neither Alice nor Alice's brother is the murderer. Then Alice's mother is the murderer.

Then, from C and D, *Alice's mother is the murderer*. (Note: It is not possible to tell who made each statement and who is the victim.)

# The Dart Game

From [1] and [2], any of six values was scored by a dart. Then, from [4], the men either scored two different values each or one man scored only one value.

If the men each scored two different values, then one man scored five 1s, from [1] and [3]. Then, from [1] and [2], each total score ends in 5 because the man who scored the five 1s scored four of a value that ends in 5 or 0. So a second man scored all the 5s (from [5], this man is Arnold) and the third man scored all the 25s. Then Buford could not have scored the five 1s because, from [3], he would have scored four 10s making his total score less than 100; this situation contradicts the assumption started with and [1]. Then Conrad scored the five 1s and his total score was either 205 (five 1s and four 50s) or 405 (five 1s and four 100s), from [1] and [2]. But then Buford, who scored all the 10s (from [5]) and all the 25s (from previous reasoning), could not have scored either total. So each man did not score two different values.

Then one man scored only one value. Then, from [1], [2], and [4], at least five different values were scored. The single value scored by one man could not have been 1 or 100 because a total score of 9 or 900 could not be scored in any other way, from [4]. The single value could not be 5, totaling 45, because at least one 50 or one 100 was scored. The single value could not be 10, totaling 90, because then (from [1] through [4]): there would be no 100s, a second man would have to score one 50 and eight 5s, and the third man would have to score 90 with five 1s and four 25s; this situation is impossible. The single value could not be 50, totaling 450, because (from [1] and [4]) a second man would have some 100s and the total of 450 could not be scored by the third man with only values less than 50. So, from [1], the single value was 25.

Then, from [5], Conrad scored all the 25s. Then, from [3],

the total score of each man was 225. For each man's score to end in 5, one man has to have 25s, a second man has to have 5s, and the third man has to have five 1s (from [1], [3], and [4]). So, from [5], Buford scored five 1s. Then, from [5], Buford scored two 10s and two 100s as well. So *Buford scored all the 100s.* Then, from [1] and [4], Arnold scored five 5s and four 50s.

# Hotel Rooms

From [2] through [6], (X) the man who lied occupied the same size room as another man. From [2] and [7]: (i) If the man who lied occupied a room that bordered on four other rooms, then that room bordered on two rooms occupied by men and two rooms occupied by women. (ii) If the man who lied occupied a room that bordered on three other rooms, then that room bordered on one room occupied by a man and two rooms occupied by women. (iii) If the man who lied occupied a room that bordered on two other rooms, then that room bordered on two rooms occupied by women.

The following reasoning uses [2].

Case I. (a) Suppose the man who lied occupied room C. Then, from i, a woman occupied room A. This situation contradicts X, so it is impossible. (b) Suppose the man who lied occupied room F. Then, from i, a woman occupied room D and, from X, a man occupied room E. Then, from [7], a man occupied room C; otherwise room E, occupied by a man, bordered on two rooms occupied by women, contradicting [7]. Then, from [1], women occupied rooms A and B. But room C, occupied by a man, borders on two rooms occupied by women. This situation contradicts [7], so it is impossible.

Case II. (c) Suppose the man who lied occupied room B. Then, from X, a man occupied room D. Then, from [7], rooms C and E were not both occupied by women; otherwise room D, occupied by a man, bordered on two rooms occupied by women. So room C or E was occupied by a man, from [1], and rooms A and F were both occupied by women. Then, from [7], room E was not occupied by a man; otherwise room E bordered on two rooms occupied by women, from [1], contradicting [7]. So room E was occupied by a woman. Then room C, occupied by a man, from [1], borders on two rooms occupied by women. This situation contradicts [7], so it is impossible. (d) Suppose the man who lied occupied room E. Then, from X, a man occupied room F. Then, from ii, women occupied rooms C and D. Then room F, occupied by a man, borders on two rooms occupied by women, from [1]. This situation contradicts [7], so it is impossible.

Case III. (e) Suppose the man who lied occupied room D. Then, from iii, women occupied rooms C and E and, from X, a man occupied room B. Then room B, occupied by a man, borders on two rooms occupied by women, from [1]. This situation contradicts [7], so it is impossible. (f) The man who lied, then, occupied room A. Then, from iii, women occupied rooms B and F and, from X, a man occupied room C; from [4], this man was Brian. Then, from [7], room E was not occupied by a man; otherwise room E bordered on two rooms occupied by women, from [1], contradicting [7]. So room E was occupied by a woman. Then room D was occupied by a man, from [1]; from [5], this man was Clyde. So, from [3], *Arden lied*.

# The Numbered Discs

From [1], [2], and [6], this axiom holds: When a woman saw two 2s on the other two women, she knew she had either a 2 or a 3 on her forehead.

From [1] through [5], as each woman was asked in turn to name the number on her forehead, each woman's reasoning in turn went like this:

| | |
|---|---|
| First woman: | I have a 2 or a 3 [from axiom]. |
| Second woman: | I have a 2 or a 3 [from axiom]. If I have a 2, first woman wouldn't know whether she had a 2 or a 3. If I have a 3, first woman wouldn't know whether she had a 1 or a 2. So I don't know whether I have a 2 or a 3. |
| Third woman: | I have a 2 or a 3 [from axiom]. If I have a 2, first woman wouldn't know whether she had a 2 or a 3 and second woman wouldn't know whether she had a 2 or a 3. [See above.] If I have a 3, first woman wouldn't know whether she had a 1 or a 2 and second woman wouldn't know whether she had a 1 or a 2; second woman would reason: if I have a 1, first woman wouldn't know whether she had a 2 or a 3 and if I have a 2, first woman wouldn't know whether she had a 1 or a 2. So I don't know whether I have a 2 or a 3. |
| First woman: | I have a 2 or a 3. If I have a 3, second woman would know she had a 2: second woman would know she didn't have a 1 because otherwise I would have known I had a 3; second woman would know she didn't have a 3 because the total is 6 or 7. Second woman didn't know she had a 2; so I have a 2. |
| Second woman: | I have a 2 or a 3. If I have a 3, third woman would know she had a 2: third woman would know she didn't have a 1 because otherwise I would have known I had a 3; third woman would know she didn't have a 3 because the total is 6 or 7. |

Third woman:
      Third woman didn't know she had a 2; so I have a 2.

Third woman:    I have a 2 or a 3. If I have a 2, each of first and second women would know the second time around she had a 2. [See above.] If I have a 3, first woman would know she had a 2: first woman would know the first time around she had a 1 or a 2; first woman would know the second time around she didn't have a 1 because otherwise I would have known I had a 3. If I have a 3, second woman would know she had a 2: second woman would know the first time around she had a 1 or a 2 [see third woman's reasoning first time around]; second woman would know the second time around she didn't have a 1 because otherwise I would have known I had a 3. So I still don't know whether I have a 2 or a 3.

(At this point no more information can be obtained by the third woman.)

Then *the third woman asked failed to name her number.*

# Finishing First

Prediction [1] has three first-through-fifth-position entrants, prediction [4] has three first-through-fifth-position entrants, and predictions [1] and [4] have exactly one entrant—Bea—in common. So all five first-through-fifth-position entrants are in [1] and [4], and Bea is one of them.

Then any entrant not in [1] and [4] was not among the first-through-fifth-position entrants. So Hal and Jan are eliminated.

Suppose Don was one of the five first-through-fifth-position entrants. Then, because Hal was not one of the five and from [2], each of Flo, Guy, and Eve was not one of the five. Then, from [5], each of Ada and Cal was one of the five. From [1], this situation is impossible because Bea was one of the five and Don was supposed to be one of the five. So Don was not one of the five.

Then, from [2] and [5], either Ada or Cal was one of the five. Then, from [1], Eve was one of the five because Bea was one of the five and Don was not.

Then, from [2], each of Flo and Guy was not one of the five because Eve was one of the five and each of Hal and Don was not.

Then, from [4], each of Ken and Ida was one of the five because Eve was one of the five and each of Flo and Guy was not.

Then, from [3], Cal was not one of the five because each of Ida and Eve was.

Then, from [1] or [5], Ada was one of the five because six of the eleven entrants have been eliminated.

In summary: Bea, Eve, Ken, Ida, and Ada were the five first-through-fifth-position entrants. So, from [3] and [5], Ada finished fourth. Then, from [1], Bea finished second and Eve finished fifth. Then, from [4], Ken finished third. So *Ida finished first*.

# The Lead in the Play

From [2] and [6], dressing room C bordered on a man's dressing room and a woman's dressing room. So (i) dressing rooms B and D were occupied by a man and a woman. Again, from [2] and [6], dressing room A bordered on a man's dressing room and a woman's dressing room. So (ii) dressing rooms B and E were occupied by a man and a woman. Then, from i and ii, (y) dressing rooms D and E were both occupied by men or both occupied by women.

From [1] and [2], there were two men and two pairs of siblings of opposite sex in the dressing rooms. Then, from [3], (z) dressing rooms A and C or dressing rooms D and E were occupied by a man and a woman. Then, from y and z, (I) dressing rooms A and C were occupied by a man and a woman.

From [1], there were only two men; so, from y and I, (II) dressing rooms D and E were both occupied by women. So, three women and one man being accounted for in I and II, dressing room B was occupied by a man.

Then, from [2] and [5], the man who occupied dressing room B was not Tyrone. Then, from [1], Tyrone's son occupied dressing room B; and, from [1] and [3], Tyrone and his sister occupied dressing rooms A and C, and one of them was the lead in the play. Then, from [2] and [5], the dressing rooms were occupied in one of the following ways (T represents Tyrone):

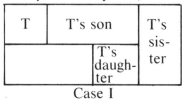

Case I

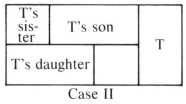

Case II

From previous reasoning, the lead was either Tyrone or his sister. From [1], Tyrone's mother occupied dressing room E in Case I or dressing room D in Case II. In either case, *Tyrone's sister was the lead*, from [4].

# The Center Card

From [1], any corner card borders on just two cards, any mid-edge card borders on just three cards, and the center card borders on just four cards. From [2] and [5], each of two aces borders on a queen; from [3] and [5], each of two kings borders on a queen: and, from [4] and [5], each of two queens borders on the same jack or two different jacks. So the queens border on at least five different cards.

There are three ways for two cards to be bordered on by a total of five cards:

Case I

```
| • | X |
|   |   |
|   | • | • |
| • | X | • |
```

The two cards (Xs) are a corner card and a mid-edge card with each of the five cards (dots) bordering on only one of them.

Case II

```
| • | X | • |
|   | • |   |
| • | X | • |
```

The two cards (Xs) are both mid-edge cards with one of the five cards (dots) bordering on both of them.

Case III

```
|   | • |   |
| • | X | • |
| • | X | • |
```

The two cards (Xs) are the center card and a mid-edge card bordering on each other with each of the five cards (dots) bordering on only one of them.

If there are only two queens (Xs), then: Case I does not apply because two jacks (dots) as well as two aces (dots) and two kings (dots) would be necessary; Case II does not apply because no ace (dot) could border on a king (dot) as required by [2]; and Case III does not apply because the two queens could not border on the same jack (dot) as well as two aces (dots) and two kings (dots).

So there are three queens. Then five cards border on two jacks (Xs): three queens (dots), from [4]; and two kings (dots), from [3] and [5]. Then in Cases I, II, and III the unmarked cards are aces. Then: Case I does not apply, from [2]; Case II does not apply, from [3]. So Case III applies and *a jack is in the center.*

From previous reasoning, the Xs are jacks and the unmarked cards are aces (J represents jack and A represents ace):

| A | • | • |
|---|---|---|
| • | J | J |
| A | • | • |

Then, because every king borders on a queen (from [3]), the top dot is not a king; so the top dot is a queen. Then, because every ace borders on a king (from [2]), the dots in the second row are kings. Then, because there are three queens, the remaining dots are queens.

# Dogs and Cats

If the conclusion in [2] is true, then the hypothesis in [1] is false; then the declarations in [1] and [2] are both true, contradicting [5]. So (i) the conclusion in [2] is false.

If Angus does not have a dog, then the hypotheses in [1] and [3] are false; then the declarations in [1] and [3] are both true, contradicting [5]. So Angus has a dog. Then, because the conclusion in [2] is false, both Angus and Duane have dogs. So (ii) the hypothesis in [1] is true.

If the conclusion in [3] is true, then the hypothesis in [4] is false; then the declarations in [3] and [4] are both true, contradicting [5]. So (iii) the conclusion in [3] is false.

If Basil does not have a cat, then the hypotheses in [2] and [4] are false; then the declarations in [2] and [4] are both true, contradicting [5]. So Basil has a cat. Then, because the conclusion in [3] is false, both Basil and Duane have cats. So (iv) the hypothesis in [4] is true.

Suppose (X) neither Basil nor Craig has a dog. Then the hypothesis in [3] is false and the conclusion in [4] is true. So the declarations in [3] and [4] are both true, contradicting [5]. So X is not true.

Suppose (Y) Basil has a dog and Craig does not. Then the conclusion in [1] is true and the hypothesis in [3] is false. So the declarations in [1] and [3] are both true, contradicting [5]. So Y is not true.

Suppose (Z) Craig has a dog and Basil does not. Then the conclusions in [1] and [4] are true. So the declarations in [1] and [4] are both true, contradicting [5]. So Z is not true.

Then (because X, Y, and Z are not true) both Basil and Craig have dogs. Then (v) the conclusion in [1] is false.

Because Basil and Duane both have dogs, (vi) the conclusion in [4] is false.

Because Angus and Craig both have dogs, (vii) the hypothesis in [3] is true.

Then: from ii and v, the declaration in [1] is false; from iii and vii, the declaration in [3] is false; and, from iv and vi, the declaration in [4] is false. So, from [5], the declaration in [2] is true and *Basil is telling the truth.* Then, from i, the hypothesis in [2] is false. Then, because Basil has a cat, Craig does not have a cat.

Whether or not Angus has a cat cannot be determined.

# The Omitted Age

From [1], let the required digits be A, B, C, D, E, F, and G as in

| | a A | b B |
|---|---|---|
| c C | D | E |
| d F | G | |

Then, from [3], either:

| Case I | Case II | Case III | Case IV |
|---|---|---|---|
| ADG | ADG | ADG | ADG |
| + AB | + BE | + CF | + FG |
| CDE | CDE | CDE | CDE |

Case I. In the middle column, A is 9 or 0. Then, from [2], A is 9. Then C is more than 9 in the left column. This situation is impossible. So Case I is not a correct case.

Case II. B is 9 or 0. Then, from [2], B is 9. Then 1 was carried from the right column. But G must be 0, so 1 could not be carried from the right column. This situation is impossible. So Case II is not a correct case.

Case III. In the middle column, C is 9 or 0. Then, from [2], C is 9. But, from [3], AB ; so C in CDE could not be

$$
\begin{array}{r}
BE \\
CF \\
+FG \\
\hline
CDE
\end{array}
$$

greater than 3. This situation is impossible. So Case III is not a correct case.

Case IV. So this case must be a correct case and, from [3], *Blanche's age was omitted from a down.* F is 9 or 0. Then, from [2], F is 9. Then 1 was carried from the right column and 1 was carried from the middle column. Because 1 was carried from the right column, G is greater than 4. Because 1 was carried from the middle column, C is 1 more than A. Because Case IV is correct and from [3], AB Then A is 1 and C is 2, or A is 2 and C

$$
\begin{array}{r}
BE \\
+CF \\
\hline
ADG
\end{array}
$$

is 3. But, if A is 2 and C is 3 in the middle column, then A cannot be 2 in ADG. So A is 1 and C is 2. Because F is 9 and G is greater than 4, B + F + G in the right column of AB must be 20 (B + F + G must end in 0).

$$
\begin{array}{r}
BE \\
CF \\
+FG
\end{array}
$$

Then, because F is 9, B + G is 11. Then, because B + G is 11 and G is greater than 4, B is 6 or less. Because A is 1 and C is 2 and F is 9, A + B + C + F is at least 18; so B is 6 or more. Because B is 6 or less and 6 or more, B is 6. Then, because B + G is 11, G is 5. Then D is 0 in AB and E is 0 in ADG. Then the completed puzzle is

| | | |
|---|---|---|
| BE | +FG | |
| CF | CDE | |
| +FG | | |
| CDE | | |

| ▨ | a 1 | b 6 |
|---|---|---|
| c 2 | 0 | 0 |
| d 9 | 5 | ▨ |

# The Hats

Of two black hats and two white hats, let X represent one color hat and let Y represent the other color hat. Then from [1], [2], and [6], either:

| | First man wore | Second man wore | Third man wore | Fourth man wore |
|---|---|---|---|---|
| Case I | X | Y | X | Y |
| Case II | X | Y | Y | X |
| Case III | X | X | Y | Y |

From [1] and [2], this axiom holds: When a man saw two (a) black (b) white hats on two of the other three men, he knew he wore either a red hat or a (a) white (b) black hat.

From [1] through [5], as each man was asked in turn the color of the hat on his head, each man's reasoning in turn went like this (R represents a red hat):

Case I
First man: I have R or X [from axiom].
Second man: I have R or Y [from axiom].
Third man: I have R or X [from axiom]. If I have R, first man would know he had X [from axiom]; he didn't know, so I have X.
Fourth man: I have R or X [from axiom]. If I have R,

|  | second man would know he had Y [from axiom]; he didn't know, so I have Y. |
|---|---|
| First man: | I have R or X. If I have R, third man would know he had X [from axiom]; then fourth man would know he had Y because third man knew he had X. If I have X, each of the third and fourth men would also know what color he had. [See above.] So I still don't know whether I have R or X. |
| Second man: | I have R or Y. If I have R, fourth man would know he had Y [from axiom]; and third man would know he had X because first man didn't know he had X. If I have Y, each of the third and fourth men would also know what color he had. [See above.] So I still don't know whether I have R or Y. |

(At this point no more information can be obtained by the first and second men. So Case I is not possible, from [4].)

Case II

| First man: | I have R or X [from axiom]. |
|---|---|
| Second man: | I have R or Y [from axiom]. |
| Third man: | I have R or Y [from axiom]. If I have R, first man would know he had Y; he didn't know, so I have Y. |
| Fourth man: | I have R or X [from axiom]. If I have R, second man would know he had X; he didn't know, so I have X. |
| First man: | I have R or X. If I have R, fourth man would know he had X [from axiom]; and third man would know he had Y because second man didn't know he had Y. If I have X, each of the third and fourth men would also know what color he had. [See above.] So I still don't know whether I have R or X. |
| Second man: | I have R or Y. If I have R, fourth man would |

know he had X because first man didn't know he had X; and third man would know he had X [from axiom]. If I have Y, each of the third and fourth men would also know what color he had. [See above.] So I still don't know whether I have R or Y.

(At this point no more information can be obtained by the first and second men. So Case II is not possible, from [4].)

Case III

First man: I have R or X [from axiom].

Second man: I have R or X [from axiom]. If I have R, first man would know he had X [from axiom]; he didn't know, so I have X.

Third man: I have R or Y [from axiom]. If I have R, second man would know he had X because first man didn't know he had X. If I have Y, second man would also know what color he had. [See above.] So I don't know whether I have R or Y.

Fourth man: I have R or Y [from axiom]. If I have R, third man would know he had Y; he didn't know, so I have Y.

First man: I have R or X. If I have R, third man would know he had Y because second man knew he had X; he didn't know, so I have X.

Second man: (Already knows.)

Third man: I have R or Y. If I have R, fourth man would know he had Y [from axiom]; then first man would know he had X because fourth man knew he had Y. If I have Y, each of the fourth and first men would also know what color he had. [See above.] So I still don't know whether I have R or Y.

(At this point no more information can be obtained by the third man.)

Then *the third man asked failed to name the color of his hat.*

# The Dart Board

From [1] and [2], each of Alma, Bess, and Cleo scored 11.

From [1], [4], and [5], Bess and Cleo cannot both have lied because both of their hypotheses cannot be true at the same time—the first person to score in the triangle is simultaneously the first person to score in the circle, and vice versa. So, from [6], either Alma and Bess both lied or Alma and Cleo both lied.

Suppose Alma and Bess both lied. Then, from [1] and [2] and the false conclusions in [3] and [4], either:

(i) Alma scored two 4s and one 3, and Bess scored one 3 and four 2s; or

(ii) Alma scored one 5 and two 3s, and Bess scored one 3 and four 2s. But, in both i and ii, the hypothesis in [4] cannot be true, from [1]. So Bess did not lie. So Alma and Bess did not both lie.

Then Alma and Cleo both lied. Then, from [1] and [2] and the false conclusions in [3] and [5], either:

(iii) Alma scored two 4s and one 3, Bess scored three 3s and one 2, and Cleo scored one 5 and three 2s; or

(iv) Alma scored one 5 and two 3s, Bess scored two 4s and one 3, and Cleo scored one 3 and four 2s.

In iv the hypothesis in [5] cannot be true. So Cleo did not lie in iv. So Alma and Cleo did not both lie in iv, and iv is not the correct situation. So iii is the correct situation and *Cleo scored the 5.*

Because Alma and Cleo both lied, the hypotheses in [3] and [5] are true; so, from [1], Alma scored one 3 in the square before Cleo scored the 5. From iii, the conclusion in [4] is true (that Bess must have told the truth is confirmed); from [1] and iii, the hypothesis in [4] is false.

# Appendix

| | Statements | | Association | | |
| --- | --- | --- | --- | --- | --- |
| | false | hyp. | 1-dim. | 2-dim. | Math. |
| Vera's Preference | | | ✔ | ✔ | |
| Speaking of Tennis | | | | | |
| Getting Married | | ✔ | | | |
| My House Number | | ✔ | | | ✔ |
| The Murderer in the Mansion | | | ✔ | | |
| The Cube | | | | ✔ | |
| Three-Letter Word | | | ✔ | | |
| Esther's Fiancé | ✔ | | | | |
| Family Occupations | | ✔ | ✔ | ✔ | |
| A Small Party | ✔ | | | | ✔ |
| The Separated Couple | | | ✔ | | |
| The Opposite Sex | | | | ✔ | |
| Truth Day | ✔ | | ✔ | | |
| The Murderer in the Hotel | | ✔ | | ✔ | |
| The Three Groups | ✔ | ✔ | | | |
| Code Word | | | | | ✔ |
| The Winning Mark | | | ✔ | ✔ | |
| A Big Party | | | | | ✔ |
| The Tennis Game | | | ✔✔ | | |
| Multiples of 7 | | | | ✔ | ✔ |
| Harry Will Marry | | ✔ | | | |
| The President | ✔ | | | | |
| Apartments | | ✔ | ✔ | | |
| Murderer's Occupation | ✔ | | | | ✔ |
| The Owner of the Table | | | ✔ | | |
| Family Murder | ✔ | | | ✔ | |
| The Dart Game | | | | | ✔ |

| | | | | | |
|---|---|---|---|---|---|
| Hotel Rooms | ✔ | | | ✔ | |
| The Numbered Discs | | | ✔ | | ✔ |
| Finishing First | ✔ | | ✔ | | ✔ |
| The Lead in the Play | | | | ✔✔ | |
| The Center Card | | | | ✔ | |
| Dogs and Cats | ✔ | ✔ | | | |
| The Omitted Age | | | | ✔ | ✔ |
| The Hats | | | ✔ | | |
| The Dart Board | ✔ | ✔ | ✔ | ✔ | ✔ |

# Index

(solution pages in italics)